Second Edition

THE CONCISE CANADIAN WRITER'S HANDBOOK

William E. Messenger

Judy Brown

Jan de Bruyn

Ramona Montagnes

Student Workbook
Prepared by Peter Chambers

OXFORD
UNIVERSITY PRESS

Oxford University Press is a department of the University of Oxford.
It furthers the University's objective of excellence in research, scholarship,
and education by publishing worldwide. Oxford is a registered trade mark of
Oxford University Press in the UK and in certain other countries.

Published in Canada by
Oxford University Press
8 Sampson Mews, Suite 204,
Don Mills, Ontario M3C 0H5 Canada

www.oupcanada.com

Library and Archives Canada Cataloguing in Publication
The concise Canadian writer's handbook. Student workbook / William
E. Messenger ... [et al.]. — 2nd ed.

2nd. ed. of: Concise Canadian writer's handbook. Student workbook/ Peter
J.W. Chambers. c2010.
ISBN 978-0-19-544709-5

1. English language—Composition and exercises. 2. English language—
Grammar—Problems, exercises, etc. I. Messenger, William E., 1931–

PE1408.C592 2013   808'.042076   C2012-908081-0

Cover images :dicapua.eu2012
Used under license from Shutterstock.com

This book is printed on permanent (acid-free) paper ♾.

Printed and bound in the United States of America.

1 2 3 4 — 16 15 14 13

TABLE OF CONTENTS

Part I: Principles of Composition

Part II: Understanding Sentences

Part III: Parts of Speech

Part VI: Mechanics and Spelling

Part VII: Diction

Part VIII: Research, Writing, and Documentation

Part I
Principles of Composition

Working with paragraphs

pp. 3–17

A. Compose topic sentences that will effectively begin paragraphs for *five* of the following objectives:

1. to explain to a ten-year-old how to make Caesar salad
2. to describe an encounter with a wild animal
3. to tell a friend about your experience of seeing an accident happen
4. to introduce an essay on the history of the European Union
5. to compare the landscapes of Alberta and Saskatchewan
6. to analyze a particular article you recently read in a newspaper
7. to introduce an essay on the role of fast food in our culture
8. to introduce a short essay about something important you learned when you failed at something
9. to explain what *Canadian* means to you

B. Write separate paragraphs developing two of the topic sentences you composed for Exercise A.

C. Analyze the paragraphs you have written in Exercise B by doing the following exercises:

1. Identify and illustrate the methods of development you used in writing each of the paragraphs for Exercise 2.
2. How did you ensure that your paragraphs are unified?
3. Identify and illustrate the techniques you used to make your paragraphs coherent.
4. What did you intend to achieve with your final sentence for each paragraph?

D. Here are some body paragraphs. Analyze and evaluate each one (you may also wish to assign rankings to them). Consider specifically each of the following principles, discussed in sections 1–7:

- methods of development
- unity
- coherence
- emphasis
- length and adequacy of development

1. Physical activity is good for people. It contributes greatly to a person's physical and mental well-being. The schedules of varsity teams are very demanding.

The swim team has eleven practices a week, of which eight are mandatory—two a day, each an hour and a half in length. The workouts consist of approximately four thousand metres each. The program also consists of running, weight training, and flexibility exercises. Not only does this sort of exercise keep a person in good physical shape, but it also increases mental awareness. Because you are up and active before classes begin, you are more mentally and physically awake than if you had just gotten out of bed.

2.   Although some people, like the members of my family, find it a mystery, doing laundry involves only three simple steps. First, different-coloured clothes take different temperatures of water: so put the darks in cold water, the whites in hot water, and the others in warm water. Secondly, you need to tell the machine whether your load is supposed to be cold or hot, so adjust the dial accordingly and put in your detergent. Last but not least, when the cycle is finished, throw your clothes in the dryer, but be careful not to dry them at such a high heat that your favourite cotton sweater becomes your spaniel's favourite jacket.

3.   "A home should be a sail not an anchor," so the saying goes. A home should provide inspiration for creativity whether this source for creativity lies in an astounding view or in beautiful and meaningful objects. A home should encourage you to look outwards as well as inwards.

4.   The storyteller makes use of animal metaphors to describe an individual's character by naming him after the animal whose stereotyped personality he possesses. The importance of living creatures in folk tales is twofold. First, the folk tale is used to teach the tribe's children the significance of individual species; and second, the use of animal names suggests a great deal about a character's personality.

5.   I am attending university so that I can learn more about myself and the world. So far I have learned that I, like Hamlet, am a procrastinator. And that the world encompasses grades, caffeine, and a few dear kindred spirits.

6.   The intertidal fauna in general and specifically tide-pool fauna can act as model systems for population studies (Raffaelli & Hawkins 1996, Johnson 2000). For intertidal organisms, the tidal cycle constitutes a major environmental disturbance, and tidal effects will be especially pronounced for protozoa, which are often abundant in tide-pools (Scherren 1900, Fauré-Fremiet 1953). Furthermore, as protozoan generation times are on the order of hours to days, they are useful model organisms to investigate population dynamics, the effects of disturbance, and cyclic behaviours (e.g. Gause 1934, Holyoak 2000). By recognizing the behaviour and distribution of these organisms, we can provide key information about survival strategies of tide-pool fauna and offer insight into general phenomena concerning the dynamics of populations and metapopulations. This study, thus, focuses on how one protozoan survives in tide-pools; in doing so we indicate the occurrence of both general and unique adaptations to a high disturbance environment.

Finding and limiting subjects
pp. 21–25

List ten broad subject areas that you have some interest in. Then, for each, specify two narrowed topics: (a) one that would be suitable for an essay of about 1,500 words (six double-spaced typed pages), and (b) one for an essay of about 500 words. (Feel free to list more than two topics if you wish.)

Examples

1. Broad topic: Clothing
   a) Narrower topics: Contemporary clothing, Renaissance clothing
   b) Even narrower topics: Gender differences reflected in contemporary clothing

2. Broad topic: Nature
   a) Narrower topics: Favourite trail walks, indigenous wildflowers
   b) Even narrower topics: The therapeutic effects of walking on trails, how to add indigenous wildflowers to a city garden

Thinking about audience and purpose
pp. 25–26

Choose a fairly simple subject (for example, your typical day at school or work, the state of your finances, your best or worst course, why you need to buy an expensive item, your health and fitness goals). Write two letters on the topic (300–500 words for each) to two distinctly different kinds of readers, for example different in age, background, education, philosophy of life, or closeness of acquaintance with you. In an accompanying paragraph, briefly account for the differences between your two letters. Did your purpose and/or style change when you changed audiences?

Generating material
pp. 26–27

Using two of your narrowed topics from exercise 9a–b, brainstorm by peppering them with questions to see how much material you can generate. Then try the same techniques with the larger subjects to see if that will yield any additional useful material. You might also want to try getting together with one or two friends or classmates and bouncing ideas and questions off one another. This is a helpful technique for preparing for collaborative writing projects.

Classifying and organizing data
pp. 27–29

Use the material you generated for the two topics in exercise 9d. Classify each mass into groups of related items and arrange each set of groups into the best kind of order you can think of for them. In a few sentences, explain why you chose each particular order. Justify in terms of your audience and purpose.

Writing thesis statements and outlines
pp. 29–34

Return to the two topics you've been working with from exercises 9a–b through 9e. If you haven't already done so, formulate a thesis statement for each topic. Make each a single simple or complex sentence. Try to compose the sentences in such a way that each foreshadows the major divisions of the outline to come. Then construct the two outlines. Make at least one of them a sentence outline. Include a statement of audience and purpose with each outline.

Revising weak outlines
pp. 29–34

One of the most important functions of an outline is to give you a graphic representation of a projected essay so that before you begin drafting the essay you can catch and correct structural and other flaws (repetition, overlap, illogical organization, introductory material masquerading as part of the body, inadequate thesis statements, subheadings that aren't really subdivisions, and so on). Here are some outlines drafted by students for possible essays. Analyze them critically; pretend that they are your own and that you'll have to try to write essays based on them. Detect their flaws, both major and minor, and then try to revise each so that it could guide you through the first draft of an essay. Do any of them seem simply unworkable, unsalvageable? If so, why?

(1) THESIS STATEMENT: Every Canadian should be fluent in both official languages.

I.   It would be good for the individual.
    A.   Improved job opportunities
    B.   Increased communication skills

II. It would be good for the community.
    A.   Increased communication and understanding between cultures
    B.   Decrease in prejudice and racism

III. It would be good for the country.
    A.   Increased nationalism and patriotism
    B.   Establishes a Canadian identity

(2) THESIS STATEMENT: Reading is a creative exercise for the imagination.

I.   Reading encourages people to visualize settings of stories.
II. Reading encourages people to visualize the appearance of characters.
III. Some plots encourage people to imagine the endings of stories or to fill in missing parts of stories.
IV. Science-fiction stories provide people with inspiration that allows their imaginations to wander.

(3) THESIS STATEMENT: The journal can play an important role in your life.

I.   Motives for keeping a journal
    A.   Keeping a record of life
    B.   Evaluating and surveying your life

II. Topics other than the weather to write about in your journal
    A.   Personal Development

      1. Health, Diet, Sports

      2. Spirituality, Dreams

      3. Books and Films, Quotes from Reviews

   B. Work Related Issues

   C. Current Events

      1. Celebrities

      2. World Events: War

   D. Travel

(4) THESIS STATEMENT: The negative effects of television on our lives

I. It leads to physical decay.

   A. People are less likely to exercise.

   B. Television encourages overeating.

II. It leads to mental decay.

   A. It requires no mental participation.

   B. People are less likely to engage in activities or hobbies that engage the mind or define their personalities.

III. It leads to social decay.

   A. People do not engage in communal activities together.

   B. People do not eat meals together.

   C. It encourages consumerism over connection with people.

(5) THESIS STATEMENT: The effects of television on our lives

I. There are too many shows pertaining to sex and violence on television.

   A. Many shows on TV lead people to accept violence as a way of life.

   B. Children are left to formulate their own opinions on sex.

II. Many people centre their entire lives on TV.

III. Advertising on TV disillusions people.

   A. Most ads deceive people into buying things they don't need.

IV. There are some good educational shows on TV.

(6) THESIS STATEMENT: Stress is a problem in university that must be dealt with.

I. Different types of stress and what causes them

   A. Unhealthy: stress overload, too much work, not enough rest, bad nutrition

   B. Healthy stress levels: small amounts of pressure, beneficial to some extent, help one learn and grow

   C. Emotional: family problems, love problems, depression, loneliness, unable to concentrate

D.   Physical: work too hard, overdoing it, too much pressure, health problems

II. Problems that arise with stress
   A.   Sustained stress: heart attacks, health problems
   B.   Common symptoms: ulcers, insomnia, irritability, sweaty or clammy hands, fidgetiness, higher pulse rate

III. Treatments: How to cope
   A.   Physical: relax, read, take up a hobby, watch TV, do something relaxing
   B.   Emotional: relax mind, meditation, exercise
   C.   Serious stress: psychotherapy, counselling, get mind away from problems

(7) THESIS STATEMENT: Safety and efficiency can be improved at Smithson's Store and Pharmacy.

I.   Layout of Shelves
   A.   Shelves in Pharmacy: the passages in between shelves are too narrow.
   B.   Shelves in Front Part of Store: there are blind spots that encourage theft.

II. Placement of Equipment
   A.   Tablet Counting Machine: there isn't enough counter space.
   B.   Compounding Area: not enough cupboard space, temperature might affect stability of chemicals.
   C.   Electric Heater: it is placed in a dangerous location.

III. Organization of Medication
   A.   Placement of medication: medication is organized by brand names as opposed to generic names.
      1.   Possible recording errors: some medications have similar names.
      2.   Stock supplies: unnecessary and space consuming extra supplies.

   B.   Wasting of Medication
      1.   Expiration of medication: some medications are hidden by the inefficient shelving technique.
      2.   Ordering of medication: too many extra supplies are ordered.

When you have finished working on these outlines, go back and examine your own two outlines from the preceding exercise. Do you see any possible weak spots in them? If necessary, revise them.

Can you think of some possible titles for these potential essays—for the ones outlined in this exercise and for your own?

Constructing and using outlines
pp. 29–34

Construct outlines for proposed essays on three of the following topics.

1. Technology has (or has not) made our lives more complicated
2. The methods you use to overcome procrastination
3. Sixteen is (or is not) too young an age at which to learn to drive
4. The steps to take to ensure a good night's sleep
5. Tattooing and piercing are (or are not) ways of making the body beautiful
6. The importance of empathy
7. The reasons why dragon myths or legends are universal
8. Why being the only/youngest/middle/eldest child in the family is the most challenging
9. If success is nothing more than one long patience (Flaubert), define failure
10. How to spend a Sunday afternoon

Check your outlines carefully for any weaknesses, and revise them as necessary.

Evaluating beginnings

pp. 35–38

Here are some beginnings from student essays. Which ones are effective and which ones need revision? Point out the contrasting characteristics that enable you to evaluate them relative to each other.

1. Leonardo da Vinci was not concerned so much with explanations of why things worked as he was with how they worked. His scientific interests were as diverse as his other interests; they covered anatomy, geography, geology, mathematics, mechanics, and physics. He dissected several cadavers and developed what are called "transparency drawings"—pictures which show both external and internal features simultaneously. He mapped several cities from an aerial perspective, and there are several entries in his notes concerning the origins of fossils and geological strata. Quite simply, he was a deeply curious man whose life shows what it means to be a true Renaissance man.

2. Problems relating to a society affect all its inhabitants; hence, all its inhabitants must take part in curing society's ills. I find that society is plagued by problems such as degenerating neighbourhoods, growing unemployment, and increasing racism. Cultural conflicts have been the root of most of our problems; thus, if the situation is to improve, some changes must occur.

3. For many people, their first thought after the ring of the alarm clock is of a steaming cup of coffee. Their stumble to the kitchen for this pick-me-up blends with their dreams. The sleepy eyes that measure out the fragrant brown granules flick open after their owners have savoured that first morning cup of coffee. After a strong cup of coffee, most people perform physical and mental tasks at the peak of their ability. The reason is caffeine.

4. The poem "To an Athlete Dying Young," written by A.E. Housman, structurally contains different periods of time in its stanzas. The different stanzas refer to different times. The rhythm of the poem is not uniform in beat. However, it has a consistent rhyme scheme. This poem is also an example of a dramatic monologue.

5. "Quit while you're ahead" may be an old and worn-out saying, but it aptly applies to A.E. Housman's poem "To an Athlete Dying Young." In this dramatic monologue the speaker seizes upon this idea as a means of consoling the athlete, or those who mourn him. Beauty and victory are fleeting. Not only does the eternal passing of time always bring change, but once our "peak" has been reached, there is no place to go but down. Rather than growing old and watching new athletes break his records, the young athlete in the poem dies at an early age. His victory garland is preserved, "unwithered," by death.

Detecting faulty reasoning

pp. 40–52

Point out the weak reasoning in each of the following examples. Identify any particular fallacies you detect.

1. She's a liberal, so she's sure to use the taxpayer's money for all sorts of give-away programs, for that's what "liberal" means: generous.
2. Your advertisement says that you want someone with experience as a computer programmer. I've had a year's experience as a computer programmer, so I'm clearly the person you want for the job.
3. Since peanuts can cause allergic reactions, they should be taken off the market.
4. He's bound to have an inferiority complex. Look at how thin he is!
5. Novels written by women often have women as protagonists. Since this novel has a woman as protagonist, it was probably written by a woman.
6. In the past, my dishwasher has always been quiet, but now that new people have moved in to the apartment next door, the dishwasher is noisy. They must have done something funny to the plumbing.
7. Dogs make better pets than cats because when they wag their tails they're happy; cats flick their tails when they're angry.
8. This critic says Mel Gibson's movies are second-rate, but since she's known to be a feminist her judgment won't stand up.
9. If I am not promoted, the company will immediately collapse.
10. Student opinion is overwhelmingly in favour of dropping the first-year science requirement. I took a poll among my fellow English majors, and over 80 per cent of them agreed.
11. The police are supposed to protect society from real criminals. When they give me parking tickets they're not doing their job, for I'm not harming society and I'm certainly not a criminal.
12. We've had an unusually warm winter, no doubt as a result of the meteorite shower last year.
13. Fashion models have slim bodies. They must be much healthier than most other people.
14. This party is for lower taxes, and so am I. That's why I am loyal to the party and always vote for its candidates.
15. People who live and work together constitute a social community, and in a democracy social communities should have a measure of self-government. Since the university is such a community, and since the vast majority of those participating in its life are students, it follows that students should have a major say in the running of the university.
16. Advertising is like fishing. Advertisers use something attractive for bait and reel out their lines to dangle the bait in front of us. They think of consumers as poor dumb fish, suckers who will swallow their stuff hook, line, and sinker. And there's a lesson for us in that: if you bite you'll get hurt, for there's always a nasty hook under the bait. The only way to protect yourself is to make sure you don't fall for any advertiser's pitch.

Analyzing arguments and recognizing persuasive techniques
pp. 40–52

1. In an essay, analyze three or four current magazine advertisements for different kinds of products. Point out all the techniques of persuasion you can find in them. Do they appeal more to emotion than to reason? Are they guilty of any particular fallacies?

2. Browse the editorial and opinion sections of a local city or campus newspaper's website. Select and analyze three or four editorials or letters in order to discover their argumentative techniques.

3. Find an online article or blog post with a large number of comments. Identify at least six cases of faulty reasoning or logical fallacies in the comments and/or article itself.

4. Find a more extended piece of argumentative writing in a magazine with national circulation. Try to find one arguing about some issue of national importance. Analyze it as an argument. Consider its subject, its audience, its structure, its methods of reasoning, its possible weaknesses, and so on. Assign it a grade.

Section 10 (3)

Including the opposition
pp. 40–52

In the following sentence outline for an argumentative essay, the student took little account of points the opposition might raise. Read through it carefully, listing as many opposition arguments as you can think of; then recast the outline so as to include those arguments. You can improve the outline in other ways as well. If you find the counter-arguments compelling, you may want to recast the thesis so that you are arguing for the other side. Include in the revised outline one or more sentences each for both a possible beginning and a possible ending of the essay. Think up a good title.

THESIS STATEMENT: In my opinion, it is better to listen to music at home rather than in a concert hall.

I.   By staying home instead of going to a concert, people save money on tickets, transportation, and babysitters.
    A. The cost of downloading music at home is a fraction of the cost of a ticket to get into a concert.
    B. Any kind of transportation is an additional cost to a music lover who goes to a concert.
        1. Cars require fuel and parking.
        2. Taxis are expensive and hard to get.
        3. Public transit is too slow and full of people who are coughing.
    C. Parents who wish to go to a live concert must hire a babysitter.

II.   Music lovers have the comfort and convenience of staying at home.
    A. They have easy access to relatively inexpensive refreshments and to washroom facilities.
    B. They can sit in an open and relaxed manner.
        1. Theatre seats are too compact and uncomfortable.
        2. The cost of refreshments is very expensive.
    C. When one is in a large crowd it is often difficult to concentrate on the music.

III.   A downloaded file provides perfect sound every time.
    A. You can listen to one piece many times using the repeat function.
    B. You don't have to listen to other people coughing, applauding, or scrunching candy wrappers.

Part II
Understanding Sentences

Subject and predicate
pp. 59–60

Identify the subject and predicate in each of the following sentences.

S   P

Example: The softball team / played horribly.

1. Carla spoke.

2. Three windows shattered.

3. Celebration ceased.

4. The three-wheeled car drove erratically.

5. The trial began.

Subject and predicate with modifiers and articles
pp. 59–60

First, expand each of the following sentences by adding modifiers and articles to the part of the sentence indicated in parentheses. Identify the subject and predicate in the new sentence.

Example: Children cried. *(subject)*

S   P

The sullen children | cried.

1. Parrots preen. (subject)

2. Citizens assemble. (subject)

3. Houses collapsed. (subject)

4. Wheat grows. (predicate)

5. Cement dries. (subject and predicate)

Sentence patterns 2A and 2B
pp. 61–62

(i)   Identify each of the following sentences as subject pattern 2A or 2B.
(ii)   Identify the subject and the predicate.
(iii)   Identify the direct object or prepositional phrase.
(iv)   Convert the sentence into the other pattern.

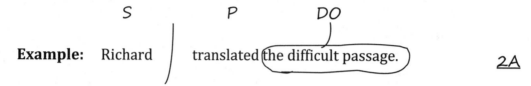

Example: Richard │ translated (the difficult passage.)   2A

The difficult passage was translated by Richard.

1.   The mischievous students submitted the invoice.   _____

2.   The fire department completely extinguished the fire.   _____

3.   We won the championship.   _____

4.   The point is argued convincingly by Nietzsche.   _____

5.   A new laptop was purchased by the generous faculty.   _____

6.   A proposal was submitted by our company.   _____

7.   Stealthy ninjas infiltrated the imperial palace.   _____

8.   The dog will be walked by Hazika.   _____

9.   The parabola is produced by a computerized function.   _____

10. I gave flowers.   _____

Sentence pattern 3
pp. 62–63

Create a sentence that follows pattern 3 using four pieces. Identify the indirect object in each sentence.

Example: I, 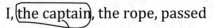the captain, the rope, passed

IO

I passed the captain the rope.

1.   I, the whole story, told, two police officers

2.   his manuscript, the publishing company, the struggling author, sent

3.   gave, her full attention, Pamela, the performance

4.   an enormous fish, caught, the professional angler, us

5.   a gourmet meal, cooked, Gurdishan, the customers

Sentence patterns 4A, 4B, 5A, 5B, and 6
pp. 63–65

Identify the sentence pattern in each of the following sentences. Also identify the objective or subjective complement if the sentence has one.

subjective (adjective)

Example: Sharon's teammates are (overzealous). 4A

1. There is one vote remaining. _____

2. Our current economic crisis was inevitable. _____

3. The judge declared the initial ruling fair _____

4. The earlier question remains unanswered. _____

5. An overwhelming majority of the student body elected her president. _____

6. Hyacinths are fragrant. _____

7. Prokofiev is a famous composer _____

8. He was painting the hovercraft yellow. _____

9. It is invigorating to run in the mornings. _____

10. You were one of them. _____

Sentence pattern 6

p. 65

Convert the following sentences into pattern 6.

1. A magnificent celebration occurred.

2. No viable design proposals exist.

3. To look directly at a solar eclipse is dangerous.

4. Ten mugs of hot tea are on the table.

5. People were everywhere!

6. Waiter, a fly is in my soup.

Do some seem better in the expletive form? Why? How might context determine one's choice?

Identifying sentence patterns

pp. 60–65

Identify the sentence pattern of each of the following sentences.

1. I gave her the envelope.   _____

2. The dangerous floodwaters receded.   _____

3. Jerome bought his niece some kumquats.   _____

4. Eleanor designated the worksite unsafe.   _____

5. There was worrying information in the report.   _____

6. The court was brought to order by Justice Singh.   _____

7. Both armies launched attacks.   _____

8. The giraffe's markings are brown.   _____

9. The pitcher shrugged.   _____

10. Orillia is a beautiful city.   _____

11. I called him an impostor.   _____

12. Her boyfriend found the current argument tedious.   _____

13. All of their children are excellent dancers.   _____

14. I admire your new jodhpurs.   _____

15. It is impossible to remember all the participants' names. _____

16. The work was completed by one of the professor's students. _____

17. Karen told me everything.   _____

18. Some of these chemicals can harm young children.   _____

19. The town council hastily appointed Olivia mayor.   _____

20. Calvin was woefully unprepared.   _____

Identifying sentence elements and patterns

pp. 60–65

Identify the pattern of each of the following sentences. Label each subject-noun or subject-pronoun (S) and each predicate-verb (V). Then label each direct object (DO), each indirect object (IO), each subjective complement (SC), and each objective complement (OC).

If you wish, also label any articles and other modifiers.

1. Food nourishes.   Pattern   _____

2. Rida finds shopping exhausting.   Pattern   _____

3. The Schmidts are excellent cooks.   Pattern   _____

4. I fix computers.   Pattern   _____

5. There are nine modules in our
    oceanography course.   Pattern   _____

6. Tamara was cured by a shaman.   Pattern   _____

7. Jacques brought me luck.   Pattern   _____

8. Certain music can affect one's emotions.   Pattern   _____

9. The group elected Jo spokesperson.   Pattern   _____

10. Some people are superstitious.   Pattern   _____

Dependent and independent clauses
pp. 66–67

Identify the following clauses as either dependent or independent.

1. she has made all the calculations correctly   _____

2. Roberto designated Jason a suitable replacement   _____

3. that was the fastest time today   _____

4. when we arrived at the night club   _____

5. because he forgot his lunch   _____

6. Although Artūrs has read most of Judith Butler's books   _____

7. while we waited for barbarians   _____

8. many pucks were stopped by Eric   _____

Functions of subordinate clauses
pp. 67–68

Identify the subordinate clause and indicate whether it is a noun, adjectival, or adverbial clause.

1. Sufjan is responsible for what happened next.

2. Ryan dived off the pier although he couldn't swim.

3. I didn't call him because I am shy.

4. The man who was our accountant lives in Calgary.

5. The town of Hazleton celebrated when Carol Huynh won the gold medal.

6. The wonderful part is that all the students debate so well.

7. The package that arrived this morning is in the mailroom.

8. What you see now is a great example of neoclassical architecture.

9. Now she understands what must be done.

10. Karl is decorating the house that Mariko designed.

Recognizing phrases
pp. 68–70

(i)   Identify each of the following groups of words as either a phrase or a clause.

(ii) Turn the phrases into independent clauses by adding missing sentence parts.

Example: the last line of the poem—*phrase*

Jacques reread the last line of the poem.

1. the complicated molecules of the structure

2. penguins survive

3. to interpret the findings of the study

4. he was recalled to service

5. for objections to arise

6. taller than the CN Tower

Recognizing phrases and clauses

pp. 66–70

Indicate whether each of the following groups of words is an independent clause, a subordinate clause, or a phrase. Label the subject (S) and verb (V) of each clause. In the case of a subordinate clause, circle the subordinator.

1. but interest rates are rising   _____

2. rarely has taxidermy reached such perfection   _____

3. for the first time in her life she was speechless   _____

4. since no one was paying attention   _____

5. down the hall from my office   _____

6. not only BC but PEI as well   _____

7. while looking for his cell phone   _____

8. his bubble burst   _____

9. after the conference was over   _____

10. according to the overly complicated directions in the book _____

Recognizing phrases and clauses

pp. 66–70

Locate and name all of the phrases and dependent clauses of three or more words in the following paragraph.

(1) Social media has created new ways for advertisers to reach consumers. (2) People who are using the web may not even know when they are being influenced. (3) One example can be found on Twitter. (4) To reach large audiences, some companies will send free products to widely followed celebrities. (5) The companies hope, or sometimes explicitly request, that the celebrity will say something positive about the product to their followers. (6) This tactic is most effective when celebrities send out a tweet praising products in memorable or funny ways. (7) What they tweet should be consistent with the types of statements that they usually make; otherwise, their followers, detecting external influence, may react negatively, which can make the advertising ineffective.

Writing appositives

pp. 70–71

Combine each of the following pairs of sentences into a single sentence by reducing one of each pair to an appositive. Construct one or two so that the appositive comes first.

1. My grandfather believes in hard work. He tends to his vegetable garden for hours every day.

2. Diana Krall is a talented jazz singer. She turns old standards into memorable contemporary pieces.

3. I must thank my teachers for encouraging me in my education. They inspired me with their confidence about the future.

4. Joe is an amateur astronomer. He uses his telescope to scan the skies every night.

5. You can save time by preparing carefully. That is, you can take careful notes and draft a clear plan for your argument.

Using appositives

pp. 70–71

Combine each of the following pairs of sentences into a single sentence by reducing all or part of one of them to an appositive. You may drop some words and rearrange others, but don't change the basic meaning. For practice, try to write some sentences in more than one way. In each case, identify the appositive phrase you have created by underlining it.

Example: Hong Kong is one of Asia's busiest ports. It is a major Pacific commercial centre.

(a) Hong Kong, <u>one of Asia's busiest ports</u>, is a major Pacific commercial centre.

(b) One of Asia's busiest ports, <u>Hong Kong,</u> is a major Pacific commercial centre.

(c) <u>One of Asia's busiest ports</u>, Hong Kong is a major Pacific commercial centre.

1. The book I read last weekend was *The Golden Compass*. It is the first volume of Philip Pullman's *His Dark Materials* trilogy.

2. To become a fine architect is not easy. It takes many years of study and apprenticeship.

3. I always look forward to April. It is the month when the cherry blossoms appear.

4. Team sports more than occupy her spare time. She plays volleyball, field hockey, and soccer.

5. Tabloid newspapers seem to go in for sensationalism. They are the smaller, easier-to-hold newspapers.

6. Canada has a larger land mass than any other country except Russia. It is a country with a small population.

7. She was relaxed and confident when she began the competition. She was sure she could win.

8. The word *hamburger* is one of the common words we take for granted. It comes from the name of a German city.

9. Dr. Snyder is our family physician. She is a dedicated person who works long hours.

10. Running marathons is not something everyone should try. It is a potentially dangerous sport.

Identifying appositives and absolutes
pp. 70–72

(i)   Identify whether the following sentences contain an appositive or an absolute.

(ii)   Rewrite each of the following sentences as two sentences by changing the absolute or appositive into its own sentence.

Example: The Vancouver Island marmot, one of the rarest animals on the planet, needs to be protected.

> (i) appositive

> (ii) The Vancouver Island marmot is one of the rarest animals on the planet. It needs to be protected.

1.   The immortal gods being not far off, our city is safe.

2.   Justin Trudeau, the eldest son of Pierre Elliott Trudeau, is now a Member of Parliament for the riding of Papineau.

3.   Mr. Twillinger, our crazy neighbour, once drove his car across our flower garden.

4.   The bay frozen, they were able to walk directly to the cottage.

5. Joseph Boyden, the author of *Through Black Spruce*, will give a guest lecture on Aboriginal fiction.

6. A music major at University of Winnipeg, my brother is giving his sousaphone recital on Friday.

7. We waited for James, Mr. know-it-all, to make some sort of comment.

8. Kamaria unhappily packed up her archery equipment, her hopes for advancing to the next round crushed.

9. My chiropractor, Waleed, suggested some new exercises.

10. We finished the dinner quickly, our stomachs full, our appetites satisfied.

Recognizing minor sentences and fragments
pp. 79–81

Indicate whether the italicized group of words in each of the following sentences is a minor sentence or a fragment. In examples where the italicized words constitute a fragment, suggest a revision to correct the problem.

1. We stayed at the picnic. *Until the sun went down.*

2. Just look at the way they play together. *How rare!*

3. You say you've never seen this man? *Never?*

4. We chose to eat at this restaurant. *It having a vegetarian menu, after all.*

5. How much wood can a woodchuck chuck? *Plenty.*

Section 12x

Recognizing and correcting sentence fragments
pp. 80-81

Identify the sentence fragments in the following paragraph. Suggest a revision for each error.

The town council of Parrsboro, Nova Scotia, has a new idea. To create a new "rockhounding" festival. Councillor Russell formally proposed the idea after she spoke with Dan McKay, who runs The Fundy Geological Museum. Which is located on the east harbour. He told her that many people come to Parrsboro to rockhound. He thinks even more would come if the town brought more attention to all of its great sites. It's true. You'll often see people down near the shore searching for fossils and minerals. Sometimes even in the winter. The town council has little doubt that a formal event could be a big draw during tourist season. Especially given Parrsboro's rich geological history. Come down for the debate and town vote this Tuesday!

Recognizing kinds of sentences
pp. 81–84

Label each of the following sentences as simple, compound, complex, or compound-complex.

1. If you read this novel, you will find yourself questioning the narrator's

    credibility. _____

2. Everybody is going to laugh on cue. _____

3. The trombonist who performed so well at this concert is the same one we saw

    last summer at the Montreal Jazz Festival. _____

4. The groom mumbled a bit; the bride spoke her vows in a clear, strong voice.

    _____

5. Few things are more pleasant than a lovingly prepared and carefully presented

    elegant meal consisting of several courses, consumed in good company, with

    soft background music, and accompanied by noble wines. _____

6. They chose the stocks they judged to be safest, but they lost money in the

    recession nevertheless. _____

7. Our classmates concluded a heated debate of the issue, and then we all voted in

    favour of lowering the voting age to sixteen. _____

8. A philosophy major will learn to think clearly and will acquire a sense of

    cultural history, and so when she graduates she should probably have the

    critical thinking skills and knowledge base to make herself employable.

    _____

Recognizing kinds of sentences

pp. 81–84

Identify each of the sentences in the paragraph below as simple, compound, complex, or compound-complex.

Additional exercises: (i) List the appositives in the paragraph. (ii) Identify the patterns of sentences 1 and 3.

(1) Margaret Atwood's early novels share similar elements. (2) Atwood submitted *The Edible Woman*, her first novel, to publishers in 1965, but it wasn't published until 1969. (3) The main character in each of her first five novels is a woman living a professional life in a modern consumer society. (4) The main character in *The Edible Woman*, Marian McAlpine, works for a marketing company called Seymour Surveys, where she is a consumer research analyst. (5) Like characters in many of Atwood's subsequent books, Marian experiences sexism, and she is forced to reassess her life when the foundation that supports her carefully constructed version of herself is destroyed. (6) After she experiences a mental breakdown, Marian confronts the predatory patriarchal society in which she lives by baking an "edible woman" cake and offering it to her boyfriend in place of herself.

Adapted from "Margaret Atwood." *The Oxford Companion to Canadian Literature,* 2e. Ed. Eugene Benson and William Toye. Toronto: Oxford UP, 1997. Print.

Constructing different kinds of sentences
pp. 81–84

1. Compose three simple sentences.

2. Compose two compound sentences, each with two independent clauses.

3. Compose a compound sentence with three independent clauses.

4. Compose two complex sentences, each with one independent and one subordinate clause.

5. Compose a complex sentence with one independent and two subordinate clauses.

6. Compose three compound-complex sentences.

Constructing different kinds of sentences

pp. 81–84

Practise creating sentences by combining the clauses below into the indicated kind of sentence(s). There are many possible answers for each set of clauses.

Example: Premier Smallwood's government and the province's two pulp and paper companies failed to negotiate a contract with one of the companies. Ladd called a loggers' strike. (compound)

> *Premier Smallwood's government and the province's two pulp and paper companies failed to negotiate a contract with one of the companies, so Ladd called a loggers' strike.*

(or, if the exercise called for complex sentence)

> *Ladd called a loggers' strike after Premier Smallwood's government and the province's two pulp and paper companies failed to negotiate a contract with one of the companies.*

1. Johann took over the family business. His sister went to university. She wanted to study philosophy. (compound-complex)

2. The ship sank. The captain drowned. The crew members stayed alive. They drifted for almost 3,200 km on an ice floe. (compound-complex)

3. Aeneas encountered Dido there. He tried to speak to her. She turned away in silence. (compound)

4. There were once wolverines throughout Southern Ontario. They are no longer present in that area. (complex)

5. Elizabeth sends Dorset overseas to join Richmond. Anne laments her misery as Richard's wife and future Queen. (complex)

6. The vertical striping common to all tigers provides surprisingly good camouflage. The vertical striping allows tigers to stalk close enough to capture prey in a final, deadly, explosive rush. (compound)

7. The business was able to stabilize its cash-flow. It expanded into the US and Britain. (complex)

8. She dislikes him. He doesn't feel the same way. He tries to deny it. (compound-complex)

9. You don't understand the problem. That doesn't matter. (compound)

10. The moving company made every effort to find your iguana. It is still somewhere in the house. (complex)

Part II: Answers

Section 12a–b (1)

1. Subject: (Carla); predicate: (spoke) **2.** Subject: (Three windows); predicate (shattered) **3.** Subject: (Celebration); predicate (ceased) **4.** Subject: (The three-wheeled car); predicate: (drove erratically) **5.** Subject: (The trial); predicate: (began)

Section 12a–b (2)

1. The green parrots preen. **2.** The angry citizens assemble. **3.** The dilapidated houses collapsed. **4.** Wheat grows quickly. **5.** The new cement dries inconsistently.

Section 12d–e

1. **[i]** 2A **[ii]** subject: (The mischievous students); predicate: (submitted the invoice) **[iii]** DO: (the invoice) **[iv]** The invoice was submitted by the mischievous students.
2. **[i]** 2A **[ii]** subject: (The fire department); predicate: (completely extinguished the fire) **[iii]** DO: (fire) **[iv]** The fire was completely extinguished by the fire department.
3. **[i]** 2A **[ii]** subject: (We); predicate: (won the championship) **[iii]** DO: (the championship) **[iv]** The championship was won by us.
4. **[i]** 2B **[ii]** subject: (The point); predicate: (is argued convincingly by Nietzsche) **[iii]** PP: (by Nietzsche) **[iv]** Nietzsche convincingly argues the point.
5. **[i]** 2B **[ii]** subject: (A new laptop); predicate: (was purchased by the generous faculty) **[iii]** PP: (by the generous faculty) **[iv]** The generous faculty purchased a new laptop.
6. **[i]** 2B **[ii]** subject: (A proposal); predicate: (was submitted). **[iii]** PP: (by our company) **[iv]** Our company submitted a proposal.
7. **[i]** 2A **[ii]** subject: (Stealthy ninjas); predicate: (infiltrated the imperial palace) **[iii]** DO: (the imperial palace) **[iv]** The imperial palace was infiltrated by ninjas.
8. **[i]** 2B **[ii]** subject: (The dog); predicate: (will be walked by Hazika) **[iii]** PP: (by Hazika) **[iv]** Hazika will walk the dog.
9. **[i]** 2B **[ii]** subject: (The parabola); predicate: (is produced by a computerized function) **[iii]** PP: (by a computerized function) **[iv]** A computerized function produces the parabola.
10. **[i]** 2A **[ii]** subject: (I); predicate: (gave flowers) **[iii]** DO: (flowers) **[iv]** Flowers were given by me.

Section 12f

1. I told <u>two police officers</u> the whole story.
2. The struggling author sent <u>the publishing company</u> his manuscript.
3. Pamela gave <u>the performance</u> her full attention.
4. The professional angler caught <u>us</u> an enormous fish.
5. Gurdishan cooked <u>the customers</u> a gourmet meal.

Section 12g–k

1. 6, no complement **2.** 4A, (inevitable) **3.** 5A, (fair) **4.** 4A, (unanswered) **5.** 5B, (president) **6.** 4A, (fragrant) **7.** 4B, (famous composer) **8.** 5A, (yellow) **9.** 6, no complement **10.** 4B, (one of them)

Section 12k

1. It was a magnificent celebration.
2. There are no viable design proposals.
3. It is dangerous to look directly at a solar eclipse.
4. There are ten mugs of hot tea on the table.
5. There were people everywhere!
6. Waiter, there is a fly in my soup.

Section 12c–k (1)

1.	2B	5.	6	9.	1	13.	4B	17.	3
2.	1	6.	3	10.	4B	14.	2A	18.	2A
3.	3	7.	2A	11.	5B	15.	6	19.	5B
4.	5A	8.	4A	12.	5A	16.	2B	20.	4A

Section 12c–k(2)

1.	1	3.	4B	5.	6	7.	3	9.	5B
2.	5A	4.	2A	6.	2B	8.	2A	10.	4A

Section 12m–n

1.	independent	4.	dependent	7.	dependent
2.	independent	5.	dependent	8.	independent
3.	independent	6.	dependent		

Section 12-o

1. what happened next. (noun)
2. although he couldn't swim. (adverbial)
3. because I am shy. (adverbial)
4. who was our accountant (adjectival)
5. when Carol Huynh won the gold medal. (adverbial)
6. that all the students debate so well. (noun)
7. that arrived this morning. (adjectival)
8. What you see now (noun)
9. what must be done. (noun)
10. that Mariko designed. (adjectival)

Section 12p

1. (i) phrase (ii) *example*: She identified the complicated molecules of the structure.
2. (i) clause
3. (i) phrase (ii) *example*: It is difficult to interpret the findings of the study.
4. (i) clause
5. (i) phrase (ii) *example*: The speaker waited for objections to arise.
6. (i) phrase (ii) *example*: The Burj Khalifa is taller than the CN Tower.

Section 12m–p (1)

1. but interest rates [S] are rising [V] (independent)
2. rarely has [V] taxidermy [S] reached [V] such perfection (independent)
3. for the first time in her life she [S] was [V] speechless (independent)
4. since [subordinator] no one [S] was paying [V] attention (subordinate)
5. down the hall from my office (phrase)
6. not only BC but PEI as well (phrase)
7. while looking for his cell phone (phrase)
8. his bubble [S] burst [V] (independent)
9. after [subordinator] the conference [S] was [V] over (subordinate)
10. according to the overly complicated directions in the book (phrase)

Section 12m–p (2)

(1) "for advertisers to reach consumers" (prepositional phrase); "to reach consumers" (infinitive phrase)

(2) "who are using the web" (adjectival clause); "may not even know" (verb phrase) "when they are being influenced" (adverbial clause)

(3) "can be found" (verb phrase)

(4) "to reach large audiences" (infinitive phrase); "to widely followed celebrities" (prepositional phrase)

(5) "sometimes explicitly request" (verb phrase); "that the celebrity will say something positive about the product to their followers" (adverbial clause); "about the product" (prepositional phrase); "to their followers" (prepositional phrase)

(6) "is most effective" (verb phrase); "when celebrities send out a tweet praising products in memorable or funny ways" (adverbial clause); "praising products" (participial phrase); "in memorable or funny ways" (prepositional phrase)

(7) "What they tweet" (noun clause); "should be consistent" (verb phrase); "with the types of statements that they usually make" (prepositional phrase); "that they usually make" (adjectival clause); "detecting external influence" (gerund phrase). "which can make the advertising ineffective." (adverbial clause)

Section 12q (1)

1. Believing in hard work, my grandfather tends to his vegetable garden for hours every day.
2. Diana Krall, a talented jazz singer, turns old standards into memorable contemporary pieces.
3. I must thank my encouraging teachers for inspiring me with their confidence about the future.
4. An amateur astronomer, Joe uses his telescope to scan the skies every night.
5. By preparing carefully, taking careful notes and drafting a clear plan for your argument, you can save time.

Section 12q (2)

1. The book I read last weekend was *The Golden Compass*, the first volume of Philip

Pullman's *His Dark Materials* trilogy.

2. Taking many years of study and apprenticeship, becoming a fine architect is not easy.

3. I always look forward to April, the month when the cherry blossoms appear.

4. Team sports, such as volleyball, field hockey, and soccer, more than occupy her spare time.

5. Smaller and easier to hold, tabloid newspapers seem to go in for sensationalism.

6. Canada, a country with a small population, has a larger land mass than any other country except Russia.

7. Relaxed and confident when she began the competition, she was sure she could win.

8. The word hamburger, coming from the name of a German city, is one of the common words we take for granted.

9. Dr. Synder, our family physician, is a dedicated person who works long hours.

10. A potentially dangerous sport, running marathons is not something everyone should try.

Section 12q–r

1. (i) absolute (ii) *example*: The immortal gods are not far off. Our city is safe.

2. (i) appositive (ii) *example*: Justin Trudeau is the eldest son of Pierre Elliott Trudeau. He is now a Member of Parliament for the riding of Papineau.

3. (i) appositive (ii) *example*: Mr. Twillinger is our crazy neighbour. He once drove his car across our flower garden.

4. (i) absolute (ii) *example*: The bay was frozen. They were able to walk directly to the cottage.

5. (i) appositive (ii) *example*: Joseph Boyden is the author of *Through Black Spruce*. He will give a guest lecture on Aboriginal fiction.

6. (i) appositive (ii) *example*: My brother is a music major at University of Winnipeg. He is giving his sousaphone recital on Friday.

7. (i) appositive (ii) *example*: James was known as Mr. know-it-all. We waited for him to make some sort of comment.

8. (i) absolute (ii) *example*: Kamaria unhappily packed up her archery equipment. Her hopes for advancing to the next round were crushed.

9. (i) appositive (ii) *example*: My chiropractor is Waleed. He suggested some new exercises.

10. (i) absolute (ii) *example*: We finished the dinner quickly. Our stomachs were full and our appetites satisfied.

Section 12w–x

1. Fragment. We stayed at the picnic until the sun went down.

2. Minor sentence

3. Minor sentence

4. Fragment. We chose to eat at this restaurant because it has a vegetarian menu.

5. Minor sentence

Section 12x

To create a new "rockhounding" festival.

Which is located on the east harbour.

Sometimes even in the winter.

Especially given Parrsboro's rich geological history.

Example revision: The town council of Parrsboro, Nova Scotia, has a new idea. *It wants* to create a new "rockhounding" festival. Councillor Russell formally proposed the idea after she spoke with Dan McKay, who runs The Fundy Geological Museum, *which* is located on the east harbour. He told her that many people come to Parrsboro to rockhound. He thinks even more would come if the town brought more attention to all of its great sites. It's true. You'll often see people down near the shore searching for fossils and minerals. Sometimes *you'll* even *see them* in the winter. The town council has little doubt that a formal event could be a big draw during tourist season, *especially* given Parrsboro's rich geological history. Come down for the debate and town vote this Tuesday!

Section 12z (1)

1.	Complex	4.	Compound	7.	Compound
2.	Simple	5.	Simple	8.	Compound-complex
3.	Complex	6.	Compound-complex		

Section 12z (2)

(1) simple **(2)** compound **(3)** simple **(4)** complex **(5)** compound-complex **(6)** complex

Additional exercises: (i) her first novel, Marian McAlpine **(ii) (1)** 2A **(3)** 4B

Section 12z (3)

1. **Example:** He had a sword in his hand.
    Example: Bronwyn leapt.
    Example: They couldn't find the missing pearls.
2. **Example:** He had a sword in his hand; he was no match for the ten-headed dragon.
    Example: Bronwyn leapt, but she shut her eyes.
    Example: They couldn't find the missing pearls; however, they did find the cat burglar.
3. **Example:** He had a sword in his hand; he had courage in his heart; he was no match for the ten-headed dragon.
    Example: Bronwyn leapt, but she shut her eyes, and she plugged her nose.
    Example: They couldn't find the missing pearls; however, they did find the cat burglar, and he looked a little like Cary Grant.
4. **Example:** Although he had a sword in his hand, he was no match for the ten-headed dragon.
    Example: After she shut her eyes, Bronwyn leapt.
    Example: They couldn't find the missing pearls though they did find the cat burglar.
5. **Example:** Although he had a sword in his hand, he was no match for the ten-headed dragon who was feeling irritable that sunless morning.
    Example: After she shut her eyes, Bronwyn, who was afraid of the water, leapt.
    Example: They couldn't find the missing pearls because they were myopic and because the cat burglar was too clever.
6. **Example:** Although he had a sword in his hand and he knew how to use it, he was no match for the irritable ten-headed dragon; luckily, nine of the knight's friends showed up at the last minute.
    Example: Bronwyn leapt, but she jumped right out again when she hit the cold water.
    Example: The cat burglar, looking a little like Cary Grant, laughed under his breath at

them, for they couldn't find the missing pearls even though the pearls were right in front of them.

Section 12z (4)

1. Johann took over the family business, but his sister went to university because she wanted to study philosophy.
2. The captain drowned when the ship sank, but the crew members stayed alive as they drifted for 3,200 km on an ice floe.
3. Aeneas encountered Dido there, and he tried to speak to her, but she turned away in silence.
4. There were once wolverines throughout Southern Ontario although they are really no longer present in any of that area.
5. Elizabeth sends Dorset overseas to join Richmond while Anne laments her misery as Richard's wife and future Queen.
6. The vertical striping common to all tigers provides surprisingly good camouflage, and it allows tigers to stalk close enough to capture prey in a final, deadly, explosive rush.
7. The business was able to stabilize its cash-flow when it expanded into the US and Britain.
8. She dislikes him, but he doesn't feel the same way, although he tries to deny it.
9. You don't understand the problem, but that doesn't matter.
10. Although the moving company made every effort to find your iguana, it is still somewhere in the house.

Part III
Parts of Speech

Recognizing nouns

pp. 90–91

Underline the nouns in the following sentences.

1. A motorcycle appeared parked in the driveway.

2. Diwali was his favourite time of the year.

3. Sharon will be reading her poem.

4. Samara gave the prosciutto to him.

5. Artifacts from the Renaissance are found in many of the world's museums.

6. Is the community centre accusing me of philistinism?

7. Toronto's largest airport, which is named after Lester B. Pearson, handles millions of customers every year.

8. My aunt, Samana, remarked that January's weather was particularly mild in her part of Canada.

9. The main reason for Claire's ejection from the exclusive club was her state of inebriation.

10. Julius read a famous novel in his introduction to Canadian literature course.

Recognizing nouns

pp. 90–91

Underline each noun or noun phrase in the following sentences and determine
whether it is functioning as a subject, a direct object, an indirect object, an object of
a preposition, a subjective complement (predicate noun), an objective complement,
an appositive, or a possessive adjective.

1. Canada's tenth province, Newfoundland, joined Confederation in 1949.

2. The Queen was given a Canadian encyclopedia edited by a distinguished
   professor.

3. Halifax's mayor presented the speed skater the gold medal.

4. We often think back with pleasure on our childhood.

5. Shakespeare wrote many plays, but *Hamlet*, a tragedy, is his best known work.

Using correct pronouns

pp. 98–101

Underline the correct pronoun in each of the pairs in parentheses.

1. (She, her) and (I, me) will start rebuilding the engine tomorrow.

2. The coach advised Anwar and (I, me) not to miss any more practices.

3. Is Tomi the person (who, whom) you think will do the best job?

4. This letter concerns (whoever, whomever) receives it.

5. There stood Eva, (who, whom) we had just said goodbye to.

6. (Who, Whom) do you wish to see?

Identifying pronouns

pp. 91–106

Underline the correct pronoun in each of the sets in parentheses and identify it as one of the eight different pronoun types. Circle any other pronouns in the sentence.

Example: Doctors (that, which, who) prescribe a patient the new drug must inform them about the side effects. _Relative_

1. We said to (ourself, ourselves, us), "The second-year students are arriving, it is time to leave." _____

2. (Those, That, Which) were the last words that Nellie McClung ever spoke to her. _____

3. Please return the whiffle balls to the coach and (I, mine, me)._____

4. The technician was very upset when he said that (whoever, whomever, who) broke the proton accelerator will have to pay to have it fixed. _____

5. To (which, who, whom) does the professor credit these insights into Virgil's lesser-known works? _____

6. The shortest poem in the forthcoming anthology is (my, mine, myself). _____

7. (Which, Who, Whom) will provide the answers to the grammar exercises if the teacher is absent? _____

8. Darrell and (I, me, my) hope our presentation will make you a little more certain about Heisenberg's principle. _____

9. People (who, whom, whose) went to different colleges never visit us anymore. _____

Avoiding gender bias
pp. 109–111

Revise each of the following sentences so that they avoid any gender bias. If the sentence is correct, place a check mark beside it.

Example: A musician is expected to bring his own instrument to performances.

Musicians are expected to bring their own instruments to performances.

1. A homeowner should always check with his neighbour before making changes near the property line.

2. Anyone wishing to register her child must bring all of the required forms.

·3. Katherine informed her brother that a professional athlete still has to pay taxes on his salary.

4. Chris wondered if any of the women in the class would take some of their time to help him with his chemistry assignment.

5. A police officer should always be prepared to recount the details of his investigation.

6. When guidance counsellors check a student's transcript, they should always make sure he has the necessary prerequisites.

Pronoun–antecedent agreement
pp. 106–112

In each of the following sentences, underline the correct pronoun for pronoun–antecedent agreement. Circle the antecedent.

1. Most presenters have had (his or her, their, his, her) research scrutinized during the peer-review process.

2. There were no theatre troupes willing to sacrifice (his, her, its, their) profit.

3. The media company opened (its, it's, their) television studios to the public.

4. If one of your boys wants to have (his, her, his or her, their) skates sharpened, you should arrive at the rink early.

5. Your convertible, like all new cars, will lose up to 30% of (their, its, it's) value after being driven off the lot.

6. The people at the campsite were prepared to have (his or her, his, her, their) tents inspected.

7. The coxswain and crew were reluctant to go out on the water after (their, its, his and their) run-in with the snapping turtle.

8. Almost anyone in the sorority will be able to cast (his, her, their, his or her) vote in the upcoming social committee election.

9. Once your group has (their, its, it's) information package, we can begin the session.

10. Neither Gary nor Mohammed saw anything wrong with (their, his, his or her) role in the experiment.

Correcting agreement errors

pp. 106–112

In each of the following sentences, correct any lack of agreement between pronouns and their antecedents. Revise sentences as necessary to avoid gender bias.

1. It is usually a good sign when a person starts caring about his appearance.

2. Una or Gwendolyn will lend you their textbook.

3. Anyone who thinks for themselves will not be deceived by advertising.

4. After studying his statements for over an hour, I still couldn't understand it.

5. Everybody is free to express their own opinion.

6. Everyone who wants to play the game will be provided with a pencil to write their answers with.

7. In order to make sure each sentence is correct, check them carefully during revision and proofreading.

Correcting faulty pronoun reference
pp. 112–117

Correct any faulty pronoun reference in the following sentences.

1. Darla trained intensely for the marathon, but it did not improve her time.

2. Will told his uncle Phil that he needed to change his shirt.

3. Summer homes make good retreats—for those who can afford it.

4. You cannot suppress truth, for it is morally wrong.

5. The deadline was a month away, but I failed to meet it, for something happened that prevented it.

6. The tone of the poem is such that it creates an atmosphere of romance.

7. Television usually shows regular commercials, but this is more and more supplanted by product placement in movies.

8. In the latest research, it says that 47% of students will require a loan to finance their educations.

Correcting faulty pronoun reference
pp. 112–117

Identify errors of pronoun reference in the following sentences and suggest a revision.

(1) Vegetarians can be divided into several different categories. (2) Lacto-ovo vegetarians differ from non-vegetarians only in that they do not eat the flesh of animals. (3) They still eat dairy products and eggs. (4) Maintaining this diet while living in Canada—a country where meat is relatively cheap and easily accessible—can be difficult, especially if the motivation is not philosophical or health-related. (5) In order to maintain a complete diet, they must pay close attention to the sources of proteins they are eating and make sure to consume enough calories, but most lacto-ovo vegetarians know this. (6) A vegetarian must find alternate sources of protein like quinoa and nuts, which are both excellent sources of protein. (7) It is a species of goosefoot and is a grain-like crop grown primarily for their edible seeds.

Identifying verb types

pp. 118–119

Identify the verbs in the following sentences and classify the verbs as transitive, intransitive, or linking.

1. Your paper's final conclusion is confusing. _____

2. Mary Fatima eats black beans and rice. _____

3. Peng harvests potatoes in Prince Edward Island. _____

4. Gabriella stopped the record from playing. _____

5. The annoying dog barked. _____

6. *The Iliad* is an ancient poem. _____

7. Our game of bocce ended in the middle of the afternoon. _____

8. The herd of antelopes scattered. _____

9. The plot thickens. _____

10. Louis Riel was outspoken. _____

11. The fire burned with intensity. _____

12. Something smells funny. _____

13. Leon tasted salt. _____

14. The board of directors will design a new plan. _____

15. This delicious wine is from Niagara, Ontario. _____

Recognizing subjective complements
pp. 118–119

In the following sentences, identify the complement of each italicized linking verb, then indicate whether it is a predicate noun or a predicate adjective.

1. She *was* sorry that he *felt* so ill. _____ (first), _____ (second)

2. Although he *appeared* vulnerable, Osman *remained* the leader for several more years._____ (first), _____ (second)

3. Because he *was* a computer expert, he *was* confident that he could write a software program for the system. _____ (first), _____ (second)

4. The book *became* a bestseller even though it *was* scholarly in its examination of black holes. _____ (first), _____ (second)

5. The children *grew* restless because they *were* tired. _____ (first), _____ (second)

6. Since the house *was* well insulated, it *stayed* warm throughout the severe winter. _____ (first), _____ (second)

7. Incredible as it *seems*, the casserole *tasted* as good as it *looked* odd. _____ (first), _____ (second), _____ (third)

8. The music *sounds* very contemporary even though it *is* quite old. _____ (first), _____ (second)

Using irregular verbs

pp. 121–125

Underline the correct verb in the following sentences.

Example: Marco claimed that he once had (<u>run</u>/ran) the 100-metre dash in under 10 seconds.

1.   My cousin has (laid, lain) on the sofa since stumbling home last night.

2.   Although she started at an entry-level position, Sally has (risen, rose) to a position of power in the organization.

3.   Before continuing the conversation, Neyha (laid, lied) her now-sleeping daughter in the crib.

4.   The forensics team determined that the suspect had (driven, drove) his car into the police station on purpose.

5.   The valley (lays, lies) to the south of Kamloops.

6.   He assumed that she should make the next pot of coffee because she had (drank, drunk) the last cup.

7.   If I (lay, lie) down on the chesterfield for a nap, could you (lay, lie) the documents for tomorrow on the table?

8.   Both sides of the conflict have (laid, lain) down their weapons.

Using irregular verbs
pp. 121–125

In each of the following sentences, rewrite the irregular verb (in parentheses), alternating between the past tense and the past participle.

1. I'm not sure what Callista (choose).

2. Children (drink) from this river.

3. Mortimer's gestures were (misunderstand).

4. The senator (stand) for different policies during election campaigns.

5. Horses (tread) this way for decades.

6. The reputation of accounting (take) its share of knocks.

7. The military (withdraw) its troops when the fighting started.

8. Native English speakers (forsake) the language's conventions.

Modal auxiliary verbs

pp. 125–128

Add auxiliary verbs in the following sentences where they are needed.

1. Perhaps we to send the letters of acceptance by post rather than email.

2. The children love to have given you a better present, but this is all they afford.

3. Nima was glad that she take her time with the assignment.

4. The current financial crisis have been avoided if investors had better understood how derivatives worked.

5. The following are ten facts about Rome that you not know.

6. Moral change occur only if the majority were to change its moral view all at once.

Verb tense
pp. 129–135

Identify the tense of each of the following sentences, then revise the sentence into the tenses indicated.

Example: The student had cheated. ___*past perfect*___ (future) (past progressive) (present perfect progressive)

The student will cheat.

The student was cheating.

The student has been cheating.

1. LeBron scored well on tests. _____ (present perfect) (past perfect progressive) (simple future)

2. Have you been painting? _____ (present progressive) (past progressive) (future perfect progressive)

3. Agamemnon broke the sceptre. _____ (simple future) (present progressive) (past perfect)

4. I am intending to prove my thesis. _____ (simple past) (future progressive) (present perfect)

5. The soldiers have new uniforms. _____ (simple future) (present perfect) (future perfect)

6. You rode horses. _____ (simple present) (past progressive) (future perfect progressive)

Revising passive voice

pp. 139–141

In the following sentences, change passive voice to active voice wherever you think the revision improves the sentence. Retain the passive wherever you think it is preferable.

1. Some went swimming, some went on short hikes, some just lay around, and volleyball was played by others.

2. The car was driven by Denise, while Yves acted as map-reader.

3. Another factor that makes the Whistler ski resort so popular is the variety of après-ski entertainment that can be found there.

4. By planning a trip carefully, time-wasting mistakes can be avoided.

5. According to scientists, it is hoped that the oil spill will be cleaned up by the turbulence of the water.

6. Record high temperatures were set in Calgary this weekend.

7. A solution was found by the school psychologist.

8. Definitions for the specific terms were contained in a legal dictionary.

Revising passive voice

pp. 139–141

In the following paragraph, change the passive voice to active voice wherever you think the revision improves the sentence. Retain the passive wherever you think it is preferable.

A substantial amount of attention was gained by Arthur Meighen for his efforts to support conscription. Because Prime Minister Borden was preoccupied with matters overseas, Meighen quickly became the most influential domestic minister. However, his approach was found too aggressive by other ministers. Nevertheless, Borden was succeeded by Meighen as prime minister in 1920. Meighen was defeated in 1921, but he briefly regained the office after he was asked by the governor general to form the government in a minority government situation. He called another election, but he was defeated in December of the same year.

Adapted from "Arthur Meighen." *The Oxford Companion to Canadian History,* 2e. Ed. Eugene Benson and William Toye. Toronto: Oxford UP, 1997. Print.

Subject–verb agreement

pp. 141–148

Underline the subject and correct verb.

1. The primary focus of this chapter (is, are) geography and history.

2. When the sun sets, the child's fear of night zombies (fill, fills) her mind.

3. The discoveries made by my student (are, is) brilliant.

4. Nearly one fifth of all indigenous populations around the world (have been, has been) affected.

5. There (was, were) a few basketballs remaining in the equipment room.

6. Only one of the guitarists (appears, appear) to be playing the right notes.

7. A centre for distressed passengers (was, were) established quickly.

8. Grazing in the field (was, were) the three cows that Josiah thought he had lost.

9. Of particular importance (are, is) Karl Marx and Adam Smith, thinkers who made significant contributions to early economic theory.

10. The crowd (was, were) singing and cheering wildly.

Choosing correct verbs

pp. 141–148

Underline the correct form in each pair of verbs.

1. Unexplained natural phenomena (fascinates, fascinate) the scientific community.

2. There (is, are) fresh coffee and muffins on the kitchen table.

3. The committee (intends, intend) to table its report today.

4. Neither Jason nor Melinda (is, are) interested in moving in.

5. Most critics agree that Timothy Findley's *The Wars* (is, are) an important Canadian novel.

6. One pair of scissors (is, are) on the table.

7. The criteria (has been, have been) clearly established in your handbook.

8. Oxygen (fills, fill) the chamber when this knob is turned.

Correcting faulty subject–verb agreement

pp. pp. 141–148

Revise the following sentences to correct any lack of agreement between subject and verb.

1. Recent studies of the earth's atmosphere indicates that there are more than one hole in the ozone layer.

2. Juliet's love and courage is evident in this scene.

3. Post-modern architecture in North America and Europe have been changing urban skylines.

4. In Canada, the media is largely based in Ottawa and Toronto.

5. This economist writes of the virtue of selfishness, but it seems to me that she, along with those who share her view, are forgetting the importance of cooperation.

6. Everything in this speech—the metre, the repetition of vowels, and the vibrant imagery—lead us to believe that this is the high point of Othello's love and, as far as we know from this play, of his life.

Adjectives
pp. 148–152

Underline the adjectives in the following sentences. Give their degree. Do not include articles in your answer.

superlative   positive

Example: The fastest car, easily turned the sharp corner

1. *The Diviners* is a wonderful book.

2. Your unfinished paper needs a more systematic defense of its initial procedures.

3. This experiment is better than Cindy and Nikki's.

4. The well-intentioned children gave their favourite teacher the shiniest, reddest apple they could find.

5. The youngest child could not swim and was afraid.

6. The gifted pianist played the sonata beautifully.

7. She took several moments to arrive at this inevitable conclusion.

8. The triskaidekaphobic professor stopped at exercise twelve.

Using articles

pp. 152–156

In each blank, place *a*, *an*, or *the*; or put *0* if no article is needed. If two articles could be used, put a slash (/) between them. If an article could be used, but need not, put parentheses around it. Some of the answers will be debatable, and we hope you will debate them.

1. _____ art books were worth _____ small fortune, but there was no space for them in _____ Centre.

2. Currently, _____ city council is divided on its decision whether to bid for _____ Olympics or to invest its energies in _____ clean water policy.

3. My sister got _____ award for her work in _____ genetics.

4. There was _____ controversial documentary about _____ drug addiction on _____ television last night.

5. I think you should put _____ onion in _____ stew.

6. In _____ Canadian society, everyone is considered _____ equal.

7. At _____ climactic moment of _____ violin solo, _____ man in _____ audience started to have _____ coughing fit.

8. After five years in _____ business, she decided to enrol in _____ International Relations.

9. In his usual exuberant style, _____ scantily clad chef smashed _____ various condiments and spices on _____ counter in front of _____ hungry and curious studio audience.

10. _____ true happiness is found within us and not in _____ external objects, circumstances, or relationships.

Order of adjectives

p. 159

Reorder the following lists of adjectives into the most natural idiomatic order.

Example: The (exceptional, Québécois, young) politician gave an inspiring speech.

exceptional young Québécois

1.   Caroline works hard to maintain her (social, extensive) network.

2.   Participants were given a stack of (circular, black) discs to keep track of their selections.

3.   Kalantha didn't like her (green, old, running, ugly) shoes.

4.   I placed the (huge, hunting, titanium) knife back in its case.

5.   Chloe spent her entire salary on a (luxurious, new, red, sports) car.

6.   The (Italian, old, ridiculous) cook wouldn't let the sous-chef do anything.

7.   Boosah bought her mother a (beautiful, Moroccan, orange) scarf for the occasion.

8.   Gary served the peas in a (china, round, small) bowl.

Identifying adverbs

pp. 160–169

Underline the adverbs and circle what they modify.

Examples: <u>Amazingly</u>, ⟨eight provinces have signed the agreement.⟩

Ricardo ⟨danced⟩ the mambo <u>expertly</u>.

1. The furniture company soon declared bankruptcy.

2. Carefully, Akiro crossed the hastily constructed bridge.

3. Sadly, Valerie's strike-out ended the game.

4. The royal caravan made very slow progress.

5. Interestingly, program participants quickly find work that is well paying.

6. Philippe almost always wins the office's chess tournament.

7. Karen seemed quite eager to learn the new security code.

8. Clive, unbelievably, just slipped the letter under the door.

Recognizing adjectives and adverbs

pp. 148–169

Underline all the single-word adverbs and circle all the single-word adjectives (including articles) in the following sentences.

1. It was hard work, so he decided to work hard.

2. Although she felt happy in her job, she decided, reluctantly, to express very forcefully her growing concern about office politics.

3. The fireplace screen was too hot to touch.

4. When the hikers were fully rested, they cheerfully resumed the leisurely pace of their climb.

5. Surely the government can find some way to raise the necessary revenues fairly.

Correcting misused adjectives and adverbs

pp. 148–169

Correct any errors in the use of adjectives and adverbs in the following sentences.

1. We enjoyed a real good vacation in the Gatineau Hills.

2. She concentrated so hardly that she got a headache.

3. The promotion usually goes to the determinedest and skillfullest employee.

4. The temperature had risen considerable by noon.

5. He preferred to wear his denim blue old jacket.

6. Nira isn't writing as good as she usually does.

7. Condos are more costlier this year than they were last.

8. The slowlier you drive, the less fuel you use.

9. He treats his closest friends worstest of all.

10. Which member of the opposition party is the more ambitious politician?

Using adjectival and adverbial modifiers
pp. 148–169

Enrich and elaborate each of the following basic sentences by adding a variety of adjectival and adverbial modifiers. Use phrases and clauses as well as single words. Try several versions of each, and experiment with placement. (Change tenses of verbs if you wish, and add auxiliaries.) Label the elements you add as adjectives or adverbs.

1. Buskers sing.

2. Politicians lose elections.

3. The goalie was hit by the puck.

4. Smartphones are tools.

5. There are lessons in childhood.

Identifying infinitive phrases
pp. 170–171

Identify the infinitive phrases and indicate their function in the sentence (noun, adjective, adverb).

Example: <u>To succeed in the game</u>, our team must put in many hours at practice.
            adverb

1.   To succeed in my classes is my most important goal this semester. _____

2.   Gisella pulled frantically on the dog's leash to keep Rover off the grass.

     _____

3.   The king eventually found a great painter to finish the church fresco. _____

4.   Because Jacqueline is so familiar with the drafting software, she refuses to use

     any other program. _____

5.   Thinking up some compelling characters is a great way to start writing your

     novel. _____

6.   Our accountant called to apologize. _____

7.   Kim is attempting to design the world's largest terrarium. _____

8.   To reflect recent advancements in the field, the scientist refined her model.

     _____

Using participles
pp. 172–174

Compose sentences using—as single-word adjectives—the present and the past participles of each of the verbs below. Then add auxiliaries and use them as finite verbs.

Example: *stun – stunning – stunned*

> She looked *stunning*.   It was a *stunning* blow.
>
> The *stunned* boxer hit the mat.   He lay there, stunned.
>
> He was *stunning* us with his revelations.
>
> He has *stunned* others before us.
>
> One can be *stunned* by a jolt of electricity.

1. interest

2. love

3. trouble

4. grow

5. change

6. ride

7. excite

8. dry

9. bake

Identifying verbal phrases

pp. 169–177

Identify the verbal phrase in each of the following as an infinitive, gerund, or a past or present participle. Indicate its function within the sentence.

Example: Waiting near the library door, Hao watched for the others.

participle — adjective modifying Hao

1. Krystoff thoroughly enjoys rowing in the summer.

2. Everyone at the dojo wanted to go to the martial arts competition.

3. Purposely distracting the other players is not fair.

4. This poem, neatly encapsulating James Reaney's work, appears in his last collection.

5. Carolyn researches cognitive psychology to understand language better.

6. The audience stared at the images projected on the screen.

7. Applying quantitative research methods to this problem will result in a much different conclusion.

8. Eventually Lyuba gained the confidence to write longer papers that were also more persuasive.

9. The poll found the majority of voters resisting the idea of changes to the education system.

10. The guy asking all of those questions must be an upper-year student.

Recognizing verbals

pp. 169–177

Identify each verbal in the following sentences as an infinitive, a past or present participle, or a gerund.

1. Coming as he did from the Prairies, he found the coastal scenery to be stunning.

2. She wanted to snowboard, and learning was easier than she had expected.

3. Trying to study hard on an empty stomach is usually not very rewarding.

4. The dinner was certain to last until midnight, permitting everyone to eat and drink too much.

5. Sent as she had been from one office to another, Cindy was tired of running back and forth and up and down; she was now resolved to go straight to the top.

Using verbals

pp. 169–177

Here are some exercises to help you become familiar with verbals and recognize some of the things you can do with them.

A. In short sentences, use three infinitives as nouns, adjectives, and, if possible, adverbs (they are less common). Then use each in three longer sentences, again as noun, adjective, and adverb, but expanded into infinitive phrases. You needn't simply build on the short sentences, but you may.

Example: to meditate

noun: To meditate is restful. (subject)

I like to meditate. (object)

One relaxation technique is to meditate. (predicate noun)

adjective: I need a place to meditate.

adverb: She cleared a space in order to meditate.

noun phrase: To meditate, feet up, before a quietly crackling fire on a cold winter night, staring into the embers, is one of the more relaxing pleasures available to human beings.

B. Compose ten sentences using present and past participles to modify different kinds of nouns—subjects, direct objects, indirect objects, objects of prepositions, predicate nouns, objective complements, and appositives.

Writing with verbals

pp. 169–177

Combine each pair of sentences below into one sentence by writing one as a verbal. Try to use a variety of different verbals. You will have to change, add, delete, and rearrange words.

Example: Farah's stories are enjoyable. They include many humorous asides.

Including many humorous asides, Farah's stories are enjoyable.

1. She had a most important goal. She would graduate.

2. Hubert went to the Chinese restaurant. He ate at the restaurant.

3. Some students protested today. They think tuition is too high.

4. Juvenile diabetes is a disease. It affects many Canadian children.

5. These days, some of my friends always talk about one thing. The only topic of conversation is marriage.

6. The test has five questions. It is necessary that you answer them.

7. Paul gave his answer. He laughed while he gave it.

8. We painted our house. It was more work than we thought.

Reducing clauses
pp. 169–177

This time reduce each italicized clause to the kind of phrase specified in parentheses after each sentence.

Example: *As she changed her mind,* she suddenly felt much better. (present participial)

Changing her mind, she suddenly felt much better.

1. Sometimes the best part of a vacation is *when you plan it.* (gerund)

2. Earning the respect of children is something *that you can be proud of.* (infinitive)

3. *Because they felt foolish,* they decided to leave early. (present participial)

4. *The fact that she had won the contest* came as something of a shock to her. (gerund)

5. The bank manager *who wore the colourful wig* started doing the samba. (present participial)

Reducing clauses to infinitive phrases

pp. 169–177

By reducing clauses to phrases, you can often get rid of unnecessary heaviness and wordiness. Practise by reducing each italicized clause in the following sentences to an infinitive phrase that conveys basically the same meaning. Change or rearrange words as necessary.

Example: We wondered *what we should do next.*

We wondered what to do next.

1. Remember *that you should be at the computer lab by 3:30.*

2. The quarterback's problem was that *he had to decide what play he should use next.*

3. My charismatic cousin gestured that we should *follow him into the restaurant.*

4. The time that you *should worry about* is the hour before the race.

5. After her motorbike came to a grinding halt, Abigail pondered *what her next move would be.*

Using absolute phrases

pp. 169–177

Combine each of the following pairs of sentences by reducing one of them (usually the first) to an absolute phrase consisting of a noun and a participle (along with any modifiers). Remember that if the participle is *being*, it can sometimes be omitted (see #12r).

Examples:

Everyone present agreed. The motion passed unanimously.

Everyone present agreeing, the motion passed unanimously.

Dinner was over and the dishes were washed. They sat down to watch a movie on television.

Dinner (being) over and the dishes (being) washed, they sat down to watch a movie on television.

1. The toddler was very sleepy. Her father carried her upstairs to her bedroom.

2. His nose was running and his eyes were watering. He sat down, hoping he had chopped enough onions.

3. The lights flickered, and the computer groaned. The 100-page report disappeared from the screen.

4. The day was breezy yet warm. They decided to take their golden retriever for a walk in Hyde Park.

5. Extra money was hard to come by. He was forced to curtail his marathon shopping trips to New York City.

Using absolute phrases

pp. 169–177

Combine each of the following pairs of sentences by reducing one of them (usually the first) to an absolute phrase consisting of a noun and a participle (along with any modifiers). Remember that if the participle is *being*, it can sometimes be omitted (see #12r). You may have to change, add, delete, and rearrange words.

Example:

The marathon was almost over. Nakita and Faye emerged as the clear leaders.

The marathon almost over, Nakita and Faye emerged as the clear leaders.

1. The fern's leaves wilted. It appeared to be dying.

2. Tonya watched her daughter dance on stage. Tonya's face was beaming with happiness.

3. Harman's head was throbbing. His hands were shaking. He didn't even know where he was.

4. On the left side of the apartment was the entrance. The door was boarded up.

5. Phil had worked with Gianna for ten years. He could not imagine running the company without her.

6. Colby's suspicions had been confirmed. He walked out without a word.

7. Emma saw the dog come over the hilltop. Its tail was wagging.

8. Jahir and Olivia's trip was nearly finished. They decided to spend their last day in Stanley Park.

Identifying prepositions

pp. 177–179

Identify the prepositions in the following.

Example: Rick Hansen started his Man _in_ Motion World Tour _on_ March 21, 1985, _in_ Vancouver.

1. Throughout our visit to the territory's capital, we made constant excursions beyond the outskirts of Whitehorse.

2. Clarissa is skilled at math.

3. While I completed the assignment, Sarah checked her email on the laptop.

4. Before you leave, please place the dirty dishes in the kitchen onto the counter beside the sink.

5. We brought all the files concerning the case except the ones with the records from January.

6. Finnegan is meeting us after class.

7. The professor requested that everyone who fell asleep during the film stay behind after class.

8. Daniel is standing near the cubicle opposite the photocopier.

9. Aziz made several calls regarding the business deal.

10. Beneath the roads and buildings lies a network of sewers, without which the city could not exist.

Recognizing prepositional phrases

pp. 177–179

Identify each prepositional phrase in the following sentences and note whether each is adjectival or adverbial.

1. Josh went into town to buy some back bacon for his breakfast.

2. There stood the famous pianist of about thirty, in the hot sunshine, wearing a heavy jacket with the collar turned up.

3. In the morning the president called her assistant on the telephone and told her to come to the office without delay.

4. The bulk of the presents was sent ahead in trunks.

5. The Siamese cat looked under the table for the ball of yarn that had fallen from the chair.

Using prepositional phrases
pp. 177–179

Prepositional phrases are essential components of writing, but they can be overdone. These exercises will give you practice both in using them and in avoiding their overuse.

A. REDUCING CLAUSES TO PREPOSITIONAL PHRASES

You'll use prepositional phrases without even thinking about them; but sometimes you should consciously try to tighten and lighten your style by reducing some clauses to prepositional phrases. Reduce the italicized clauses in the following sentences to prepositional phrases. Revise in other ways as well if you wish, but don't change the essential meaning.

Example: The cold front *that is over the coast* will move inland overnight.

The cold front over the coast will move inland overnight.

1. *If you have enough stamina,* you can take part in the triathlon.

2. *Because she was so confident,* she entered every race.

3. Students *who have part-time jobs* must budget their time carefully.

4. We need advice *that only a grandmother can give us.*

5. *The time when you should eat* is three hours before you go to sleep.

B. REDUCING CLAUSES TO PREPOSITIONAL PHRASES USING GERUNDS

Gerunds (see #21f–g) are often used as objects of prepositions. Convert the italicized clauses in the following sentences to prepositional phrases with gerunds.

Example: *Before she submitted the essay*, she proofread it carefully.

Before submitting the essay, she proofread it carefully.

1. *When I had run* only half a block, I felt exhausted.

2. *Although Petra trained rigorously*, she didn't get past the preliminaries.

3. You can't hope to understand *unless you attend all the classes.*

4. *They checked the luggage carefully* and found nothing but a pair of toenail clippers.

5. He deserves some credit *because he tried so hard.*

C. GETTING RID OF EXCESSIVE PREPOSITIONAL PHRASES

When prepositional phrases come in bunches, they can contribute to wordiness. Practise revising to get rid of clutter: cut the number of prepositional phrases in each of the following sentences (shown in parentheses) at least in half.

Example: Some of the ministers in the Cabinet are in danger of losing their appointments because of the poor quality of their relations with the media and deficits in their department budgets. (8)

Because they have poor media relations and departmental budget deficits, some Cabinet ministers may lose their appointments. (8 prepositional phrases reduced to 0)

1. Sarah got to the top of the mountain first by using several trails unknown to her competitors in the race, which was held during the celebration of the centennial of the province's entry into confederation. (9)

2. The feeling of most of the people at the meeting was that the committee chair spoke in strident tones for too long about things about which he knew little. (7)

3. The irritated ghost at the top of the stairs of the old house shouted at me to get away from his door in a hurry. (6)

4. One of the most respected of modern historians has some odd ideas about the beginning of the war between European nations that broke out, with such devastating consequences, in early August of 1914. (8)

5. Economists' predictions about the rise and fall of interest rates seem to be accurate for the most part, but only within the limits of a period of about three or four weeks, at most, and even at that you have to take them with a grain of salt. (10)

Using coordinating conjunctions
pp. 181–184

Put an appropriate coordinating conjunction in each blank. If more than one is possible, list the alternative words in parentheses.

1. Uma was late for the meeting, _____ she had a good excuse.

2. There is only one solution to this problem, _____ I know what it is.

3. No one likes noise pollution, _____ some people insist that we have to live with it.

4. Her brother is not cynical, _____ is he insensitive.

5. We were puzzled by the professor's humorous comments, _____ we had expected her to speak seriously on the subject.

6. The tuba solo came as a surprise, _____ Tomas and Uli were expecting an organ concerto.

7. She had two choices: she could fasten the component with rivets, _____ she could create a new design.

8. Theoretical developments are not neatly insulated from one another, _____ are they arranged in neat phases.

Recognizing subordinate clauses

pp. 186–188

Identify the subordinate clauses in the following passage and indicate how each is functioning: as adjective, adverb, or noun. (Remember that sometimes relative pronouns are omitted; see #14d and #43f.) What words do the adjectival and adverbial clauses modify? How does each noun clause function? (You might begin by identifying the *independent* clauses.)

(1) Once upon a time, when he was only eight, Selwyn decided he wanted to be a marine biologist. (2) He especially liked to play in the numerous tide pools found outside the Peggy's Cove cabin where his family stayed every summer. (3) As he grew older, he discovered that in order to become a marine biologist, one had to study many different and difficult subjects that seemed far removed from ocean life. (4) Whenever he worked on his math, statistics, or computer problems in stuffy rooms, he kept longing to walk on the beach. (5) That he became a successful field scientist and expert on the microorganisms found in tide pools is, therefore, not surprising. (6) What most people don't know is that when Selwyn became a full professor, he didn't need to worry about doing analysis anymore because he had graduate students who enjoyed working with numbers and who derived satisfaction from developing new approaches to data analysis. (7) So while they crunched numbers, Selwyn puttered around happily ever after on shorelines all over the world looking deep into tide pools.

Using subordinating conjunctions
pp. 186–188

Combine each pair of sentences below into a single complex sentence by using the subordinating conjunction supplied in parentheses. You will have to change, add, delete, and rearrange words in some cases. Try rearranging the order of clauses in some of your answers.

Example: We knew some parents would demand the inclusion of Latin in the curriculum. They voted against the new measure. (who)

> *The parents who we knew would demand the inclusion of Latin in the curriculum voted against the new measure.*

1. Ida is training very hard. She wants to go to the olympics. (because)

2. They went to the museum. Next, they stopped for lunch. (after)

3. We included an extra key. You lose the other one. (in case)

4. Corporations will pollute the oceans. We need to create stronger government regulations. (unless)

5. You haven't brought your registration. You will have to wait in line. (if)

6. Annie thinks she should work on commission. Her boss thinks Annie should be paid hourly. (whereas)

7. Harold waited. Karen arrived. (until)

8. We brought the hammocks. The cottage didn't have any trees. (where)

Writing subordinate clauses

pp. 186–188

Combine each of the following pairs of simple sentences into a single complex sentence by subordinating one clause and attaching it to the other with one of the subordinators listed on page 187. You may want to change, delete, or add some words, reverse the clauses, or otherwise rearrange words. Experiment with different subordinators.

Example: The technological revolution has affected many business and professional people. Its largest impact may prove to have been on the young.

> *(Though, Although) the technological revolution has affected many business and professional people, its . . .*

> *The technological revolution has affected many business and professional people, (though, even though) its . . .*

1. The art gallery won't open until next week. The leak in the roof hasn't been repaired yet.

2. Canada's gun laws are still stricter than those in the United States. We should defend this.

3. Some students may not have paid all their fees. They would not yet be considered officially registered.

4. First you should master the simple sentence. Then you can work on rhyming couplets.

5. The children ate most of their Halloween candy. They are bouncing off the walls.

Identifying conjunctions
pp. 181–188

Underline the conjunctions in the following. Indicate their type.

(1) Hart A. Massey, a successful manufacturer of agricultural farm equipment, bought land at the corner of Shuter and Victoria in 1892 to build an auditorium. (2) His inspiration contained some poignancy, for he planned the building as a memorial to his son. (3) The project was costly, but he intended it would become a famous facility like New York's Carnegie Hall or London's Royal Albert Hall. (4) After construction was completed in 1894, Massey Music Hall opened its doors. (5) Since its first performance, Handel's *Messiah*, the hall has not only presented thousands of concerts, but also hosted various other events including weddings, boxing matches, chess tournaments, and even typing contests. (6) Many famous people have stood on its stage, including Winston Churchill, Charlie Parker, Maria Callas, and Bob Marley. (7) It continues to be a popular venue for many performers whenever they stop in Toronto.

With information from Kilbourn, W. *Intimate Grandeur: One Hundred Years at Massey Hall.* Toronto: Stoddart Publishing, 1993. Print.

Writing with conjunctions

pp. 181–188

Combine each pair of sentences twice using the type of conjunction indicated. Try to write the most efficient sentence possible. You may not have to rewrite all of both clauses in your answer.

Example: We returned to the cabin. Our dinner was ready. (subordinating)

We returned to the cabin because our dinner was ready.

Example: Mark is strong. Mark is fast. (coordinating)

Mark is strong and fast.

1. She led the team in assists. She lead the team in goals. (correlative)

2. Winter started late this year. Spring started early. (coordinating)

3. *Hamlet* could have been written in 1601. *Hamlet* could have been written in 1602. (coordinating)

4. The ballerinas returned to the stage. The crowd applauded. (subordinating)

5. Hiroto will make you sashimi. Teru will make you steak. (correlative)

6. The Rosetta stone is an amazing object. Who owns it? (coordinating)

7. The carnival ended. The Ferris wheel broke down. (subordinating)

8. You enrolled in physics. You do not have to enrol in math. (coordinating)

9. The judges were impressed. The other divers were impressed. (correlating)

10. The turtle swam across the aquarium. The biologist marked it in her records. (coordinating)

Recognizing parts of speech

pp. 87–188

Identify the part of speech of each word in the following sentences.

1. The lazy boatman was sleeping, so she boldly crossed the river herself.

2. Since she became a manager, Jelina hardly talks to us anymore.

3. Alas, I cannot present my paper in class this Saturday.

4. Deadly wildfires devastate the Australian countryside.

5. We knew each other before the war, but we never spoke.

6. Sabastian recited his litany of worsening facts and figures, including the latest hunger statistics.

7. A large raccoon quietly invaded the cottage because it sensed food inside.

8. Whoever left these potato chips on the floor will suffer serious consequences when I find him.

9. They just figured that because he was from another country hockey would be foreign to him.

10. We travelled on large boats for years, but travelling on a train is a completely new experience to my brother and me.

Recognizing and using parts of speech

pp. 87–188

A. RECOGNIZING PARTS OF SPEECH

To test yourself, see if you can identify the part of speech of each word in the following sentences. Can you say how each is functioning grammatically? What kinds of sentences are they?

1. The skyline of modern Toronto provides a striking example of what modern architecture can do to distinguish a major city.

2. Waiter, there's a fly doing the back crawl in my soup!

3. Well, to tell the truth, I just did not have the necessary patience!

4. Why should anyone be unhappy about paying a fair tax?

5. Neither the captain nor the crew could be blamed for the terribly costly ferry accident.

6. The elevator business has been said to have its ups and downs.

7. Don, please put back the chocolate cake.

8. While abroad, I learned to manage with only three large suitcases and one full-time chauffeur.

9. In a few seconds, the computer told us much more than we needed to know.

10. Help!

B. USING DIFFERENT PARTS OF SPEECH

For fun, write some sentences using the following words as different parts of speech—as many different ones as you can. Each word can function as at least two different parts of speech.

shed	still	round
best	train	set
left	cover	rose
plant	wrong	cross
before	last	near

Part III: Answers

Section 13b (1)

1. A <u>motorcycle</u> appeared parked in the <u>driveway</u>.
2. <u>Diwali</u> was his favourite <u>time</u> of the <u>year</u>.
3. <u>Sharon</u> will be reading her <u>poem</u>.
4. <u>Samara</u> gave the <u>prosciutto</u> to him.
5. <u>Artifacts</u> from the <u>Renaissance</u> are found in many of the <u>world's</u> <u>museums</u>.
6. Is the <u>community centre</u> accusing me of philistinism?
7. <u>Toronto's</u> largest <u>airport</u>, which is named after <u>Lester B. Pearson</u>, handles <u>millions</u> of <u>customers</u> every <u>year</u>.
8. My <u>aunt</u>, <u>Samana</u>, remarked that <u>January's</u> <u>weather</u> was particularly mild in her <u>part</u> of <u>Canada</u>.
9. The main <u>reason</u> for <u>Claire's</u> <u>ejection</u> from the exclusive <u>club</u> was her <u>state</u> of <u>inebriation</u>.
10. <u>Julius</u> read a famous <u>novel</u> in his <u>introduction</u> to Canadian <u>literature</u> <u>course</u>.

Section 13b (2)

1. <u>Canada's</u> tenth <u>province</u>, <u>Newfoundland</u>, joined <u>Confederation</u> in <u>1949</u>.

   Canada's: possessive adjective
   province: subject
   Newfoundland: appositive
   Confederation: direct object
   1949: object of a preposition (in)

2. The <u>Queen</u> was given a Canadian <u>encyclopedia</u> edited by a distinguished <u>professor</u>.

   Queen: subject
   encyclopedia: direct object
   professor: object of a preposition (by)

3. <u>Halifax's</u> <u>mayor</u> presented the speed <u>skater</u> the gold <u>medal</u>.

   Halifax's: possessive adjective
   mayor: subject
   skater: indirect object
   medal: direct object

4. We often think back with <u>pleasure</u> on our <u>childhood</u>.

   pleasure: object of a preposition (with)
   childhood: object of a preposition (on)

5. <u>Shakespeare</u> wrote many <u>plays</u>, but <u>Hamlet</u>, a <u>tragedy</u>, is his best known <u>work</u>.

   Shakespeare: subject
   plays: direct object
   ***Hamlet*: subject**
   tragedy: appositive
   work: subjective complement

Section 14e

1. <u>She</u> and <u>I</u> will start rebuilding the engine tomorrow.

2. The coach advised Anwar and <u>me</u> not to miss any more practices.
3. Is Tomi the person <u>who</u> you think will do the best job?
4. This letter concerns <u>whoever</u> receives it.
5. There stood Eva, <u>whom</u> we had just said goodbye to.
6. <u>Whom</u> do you wish to see?

Section 14

1. <u>We</u> said to (ourself, <u>ourselves</u>, us), "The second-year students are arriving, <u>it</u> is time to leave." (reflexive)
2. (<u>Those</u>, That, Which) were the last words that Nellie McClung ever spoke to <u>her</u>. (demonstrative)
3. Please return the whiffle balls to the coach and (I, mine, <u>me</u>). (personal)
4. The technician was very upset when <u>he</u> said that (<u>whoever</u>, whomever, who) broke the proton accelerator will have to pay to have <u>it</u> fixed. (relative)
5. To (which, who, <u>whom</u>) does the professor credit <u>these</u> insights into Virgil's lesser-known works? (interrogative)
6. The shortest poem in the forthcoming anthology is (my, <u>mine</u>, myself). (personal)
7. (Which, <u>Who</u>, Whom) will provide the answers to the grammar exercises if the teacher is absent? (interrogative)
8. Darrell and (<u>I</u>, me, my) hope our presentation will make <u>you</u> a little more certain about Heisenberg's principle. (personal)
9. People (<u>who</u>, whom, whose) went to different colleges never visit <u>us</u> anymore. (relative)

Section 15d

1. Homeowners should always check with their neighbours before making changes near the property line.
2. People who wish to register their children must bring all of the required forms.
3. Katherine informed her brother that professional athletes still have to pay taxes on their salaries.
4. No revision necessary.
5. Police officers should always be prepared to recount the details of their investigations.
6. When guidance counsellors check student transcripts, they should always make sure the necessary prerequisites are there.

Section 15 (1)

1. Most <u>presenters</u> have had (his or her, <u>their</u>, his, her) research scrutinized during the peer-review process.
2. There were no theatre <u>troupes</u> willing to sacrifice (his, her, its, <u>their</u>) profit.
3. <u>The media company</u> opened (<u>its</u>, it's, their) television studios to the public.
4. If <u>one of your boys</u> wants to have (<u>his</u>, her, his or her, their) skates sharpened, you should arrive at the rink early.
5. <u>Your convertible</u>, like all new cars, will lose up to 30% of (their, <u>its</u>, it's) value after being driven off the lot.
6. <u>The people</u> at the campsite were prepared to have (his or her, his, her, <u>their</u>) tents inspected.
7. <u>The coxswain and crew</u> were reluctant to go out on the water after (<u>their</u>, its, his and

their) run-in with the snapping turtle.

8. Almost <u>anyone</u> in the sorority will be able to cast (his, <u>her</u>, their, his or her) vote in the upcoming social committee election.

9. Once your <u>group</u> has (their, <u>its</u>, it's) information package, we can begin the session.

10. <u>Neither</u> Gary nor Mohammed saw anything wrong with (their, <u>his</u>, his or her) role in the experiment.

Section 15 (2)

1. It is usually a good sign when **a person** starts caring about **his** [or **her**] appearance.

2. Una or Gwendolyn will lend you **her** textbook.

3. **Those** who think for **themselves** will not be deceived by advertising.
   Anyone who thinks for **himself** [or **herself**] will not be deceived by advertising.

4. After studying his **statements** for over an hour, I still couldn't understand **them**.

5. **Everybody** is free to express **his** [or **her**] own opinion.
   Everybody is free to express **an** opinion.
   We are each free to express **our** own opinion.

6. Everyone who wants to play the game will be provided with a pencil to write **answers** with.
   Everyone who wants to play the game will be provided with a pencil to write **his** [or **her**] answers with.

7. In order to make sure each sentence is correct, **check carefully** during revision and proofreading.
   In order to make sure **all sentences** are correct, check **them** carefully during revision and proofreading.

Section 16 (1)

1. Darla trained intensely for the marathon, but **her efforts** did not improve her time.

2. Will **told his uncle Phil to change his shirt**
   Will said, "Uncle Phil, I need to change my shirt."

3. Summer homes—for those who can afford **them**—make good retreats.

4. You cannot suppress truth, for **to do so** is morally wrong.
   You cannot suppress truth, for **doing so** is morally wrong.
   You cannot suppress truth, for **that** is morally wrong.

5. The deadline was a month away, but I failed to meet it, for something happened to prevent **me from completing my application on time.**

6. The tone of the poem **creates an atmosphere of romance.**
   The tone of the poem is such that **it (the tone)** creates an atmosphere of romance.

7. Television usually shows regular commercials, but **this kind of advertising** is more and more supplanted by product placement in movies.

8. **The latest research says** that 47% of students will require a loan to finance their educations.
   According to the latest research, 47% of students will require a loan to finance their educations.

Section 16 (2)

(5) In order to maintain a complete diet, *they* must pay close attention to the sources of proteins they are eating and make sure to consume enough calories, but most vegetarians know *this*.

"they" = remote antecedent

"this" = vague reference

Revision: In order to maintain a complete diet, *lacto-ovo vegetarians* must pay close attention to the sources of proteins they are eating and make sure to consume enough calories, but most vegetarians know about *these requirements*.

(7) *It* is a species of goosefoot and is a grain-like crop grown primarily for *their* edible seeds.

"it" = ambiguous reference

"their" = lack of agreement with antecedent ("crop")

Revision: *Quinoa* comes from a species of goosefoot, and is a grain-like crop grown primarily for *its* edible seeds.

Section 17a (1)

1. Your paper's final conclusion <u>is</u> confusing. (linking)
2. Mary Fatima <u>eats</u> black beans and rice. (transitive)
3. Peng <u>harvests</u> potatoes in Prince Edward Island. (transitive)
4. Gabriella <u>stopped</u> the record from playing. (transitive)
5. The annoying dog <u>barked</u>. (intransitive)
6. *The Iliad* <u>is</u> an ancient poem. (linking)
7. Our game of bocce <u>ended</u> in the middle of the afternoon. (intransitive)
8. The herd of antelopes <u>scattered</u>. (intransitive)
9. The plot <u>thickens</u>. (intransitive)
10. Louis Riel <u>was</u> outspoken. (linking)
11. The fire <u>burned</u> with intensity. (intransitive)
12. Something <u>smells</u> funny. (linking)
13. Leon <u>tasted</u> salt. (transitive)
14. The board of directors <u>will design</u> a new plan. (transitive)
15. This delicious wine <u>is</u> from Niagara, Ontario. (linking)

Section 17a (2)

1. She *was* <u>sorry</u> that he *felt* so <u>ill</u>.
   sorry: predicate adjective
   ill: predicate adjective
2. Although he *appeared* <u>vulnerable</u>, Osman *remained* the <u>leader</u> for several more years.
   vulnerable: predicate adjective
   leader: predicate noun
3. Because he *was* a computer <u>expert</u>, he *was* <u>confident</u> that he could write a software program for the system.
   expert: predicate noun
   confident: predicate adjective
4. The book *became* a <u>bestseller</u> even though it *was* <u>scholarly</u> in its examination of black holes.

bestseller: predicate noun
scholarly: predicate adjective

5. The children *grew* <u>restless</u> because they *were* <u>tired</u>.

 restless: predicate adjective
 tired: predicate adjective

6. Since the house *was* well <u>insulated</u>, it *stayed* <u>warm</u> throughout the severe winter.

 insulated: predicate adjective
 warm: predicate adjective

7. <u>Incredible</u> as it *seems*, the casserole *tasted* as <u>good</u> as it *looked* <u>odd</u>.

 incredible: predicate adjective
 good: predicate adjective
 odd: predicate adjective

8. The music *sounds* very <u>contemporary</u> even though it *is* quite <u>old</u>.

 contemporary: predicate adjective
 old: predicate adjective

Section 17c (1)

1. lain **2.** risen **3.** laid **4.** driven **5.** lies **6.** drunk **7.** lie; lay **8.** laid

Section 17c (2)

1. I'm not sure what Callista chose. I'm not sure what Callista has chosen.
2. Children drank from this river. Children have drunk from this river.
3. Mortimer's gestures were misunderstood. Mortimer's gestures had been misunderstood.
4. The senator stood for different policies during election campaigns. The senator has stood for different policies during election campaigns.
5. Horses trod this way for decades. Horses have trodden/trod this way for decades.
6. The reputation of accounting took its share of knocks. The reputation of accounting has taken its share of knocks.
7. The military withdrew its troops when the fighting started. The military had withdrawn its troops when the fighting started.
8. Native English speakers forsook the language's conventions. Native English speakers have forsaken the language's conventions.

Section 17e

1. Perhaps we **ought** to send the letters of acceptance by post rather than email.
2. The children **would** love to have given you a better present, but this is all they **could** afford.
3. Nima was glad that she **could** take her time with the assignment.
4. The current financial crisis **might [not 'may']** have been avoided if investors had better understood how derivatives worked.
5. The following are ten facts about Rome that you **may** not know.
6. Moral change **could** occur only if the majority were to change its moral view all at once.

Section 17g

1. Simple past. LeBron has scored well on tests. LeBron had been scoring well on tests. LeBron will score well on tests.
2. Present perfect progressive. Are you painting? Were you painting? Will you have been painting?
3. Simple past. Agamemnon will break the sceptre. Agamemnon is breaking the sceptre. Agamemnon had broken the sceptre.
4. Present progressive. I intended to prove my thesis. I will be intending to prove my thesis. I have intended to prove my thesis.
5. Present. The soldiers will have new uniforms. The soldiers have had new uniforms. The soldiers will have had new uniforms.
6. Past. You were riding horses. You will have ridden horses. You rode horses.

Section 17-I (1)

1. Some went swimming, some went on short hikes, some just lay around, and others played volleyball.
2. Denise drove the car, while Yves acted as map-reader.
3. Retain the passive voice in this sentence.
4. By planning a trip carefully, you can avoid time-wasting mistakes.
5. Scientists hope that the turbulence of the water will clean up the oil spill.
6. Retain the passive voice in this sentence.
7. The school psychologist found a solution.
8. A legal dictionary contained definitions of the specific terms.

Section 17-I (2)

Arthur Meighen gained a substantial amount of attention for his efforts to support conscription. Because Prime Minister Borden was preoccupied with matters overseas, Meighen quickly became the most influential domestic minister. However, *other ministers found his approach too aggressive.* Nevertheless, *Meighen succeeded Borden as prime minister* in 1920. Meighen was defeated in 1921, but he briefly regained the office *after the governor general asked him to* form the government in a minority government situation. He called another election, but he was defeated in December of the same year.

Section 18 (1)

1. <u>The primary focus</u> of this chapter (<u>is</u>/are) geography and history.
2. When the sun sets, the child's <u>fear</u> of night zombies (fill/<u>fills</u>) her mind.
3. <u>The discoveries</u> made by my student (<u>are</u>/is) brilliant.
4. Nearly <u>one fifth</u> of all indigenous populations around the world (have been/<u>has been</u>) affected.
5. There (was/<u>were</u>) <u>a few basketballs</u> remaining in the equipment room.
6. Only <u>one</u> of the guitarists (<u>appears</u>/appear) to be playing the right notes.
7. <u>A centre</u> for distressed passengers (<u>was</u>/were) established quickly.
8. Grazing in the field (was/<u>were</u>) <u>the three cows</u> that Josiah thought he had lost.
9. Of particular importance (<u>are</u>/is) <u>Karl Marx and Adam Smith,</u> thinkers who made significant contributions to early economic theory.

10. The crowd (was/were) singing and cheering wildly.

Section 18 (2)

1. Unexplained natural phenomena <u>fascinate</u> the scientific community.
2. There <u>is</u> fresh coffee and muffins on the kitchen table.
3. The committee <u>intends</u> to table its report today.
4. Neither Jason nor Melinda <u>is</u> interested in moving in.
5. Most critics agree that Timothy Findley's *The Wars* <u>is</u> an important Canadian novel.
6. One pair of scissors <u>is</u> on the table.
7. The criteria <u>have been</u> clearly established in your handbook.
8. Oxygen <u>fills</u> the chamber when this knob is turned.

Section 18 (3)

1. Recent studies of the earth's atmosphere <u>indicate</u> that there <u>is</u> more than one hole in the ozone layer.
2. Juliet's love and courage <u>are</u> evident in this scene.
3. Post-modern architecture in North America and Europe <u>has</u> been changing urban skylines.
4. In Canada, the media <u>are</u> largely based in Ottawa and Toronto.
5. This economist writes of the virtue of selfishness, but it seems to me that she, along with those who share her view, <u>is</u> forgetting the importance of cooperation.
6. Everything in this speech—the metre, the repetition of vowels, and the vibrant imagery—<u>leads</u> us to believe that this is the high point of Othello's love and, as far as we know from this play, of his life.

Section 19a–b

1. *The Diviners* is a <u>wonderful</u> book. (positive)
2. Your <u>unfinished</u> paper needs a <u>more systematic</u> defense of its <u>initial</u> procedures. (positive, comparative, positive)
3. This experiment is <u>better</u> than Cindy and Nikki's. (comparative)
4. The <u>well-intentioned</u> children gave their <u>favourite</u> teacher the <u>shiniest</u>, <u>reddest</u> apple they could find. (positive, positive, superlative, superlative)
5. The <u>youngest</u> child could not swim and was <u>afraid</u>. (superlative, positive)
6. The <u>gifted</u> pianist played the sonata beautifully. (positive)
7. She took <u>several</u> moments to arrive at this <u>inevitable</u> conclusion. (positive, positive)
8. The <u>triskaidekaphobic</u> professor stopped at exercise twelve. (positive)

Section 19c

1. ***The*** art books were worth ***a*** small fortune, but there was no space for them in ***the*** Centre.
2. Currently, ***the*** city council is divided on its decision whether to bid for ***the*** Olympics or to invest its energies in ***(a)*** clean water policy.
3. My sister got ***an/the*** award for her work in ***0*** genetics.
4. There was ***a*** controversial documentary about ***0*** drug addiction on ***0*** television last night.
5. I think you should put ***an*** onion in ***the*** stew.

6. In _**0**_ Canadian society, everyone is considered _**(an)**_ equal.
7. At _**the/a**_ climactic moment of _**the**_ violin solo, _**a/the**_ man in _**the**_ audience started to have _**a**_ coughing fit.
8. After five years in _**0**_ business, she decided to enrol in _**0**_ International Relations.
9. In his usual exuberant style, _**the**_ scantily clad chef smashed _**(the)**_ various condiments and spices on _**the**_ counter in front of _**the**_ hungry and curious studio audience.
10. _**0**_ True happiness is found within us and not in _**0**_ external objects, circumstances, or relationships.

Section 19e

1. Extensive social
2. Black circular [or] circular black
3. ugly old green running
4. huge titanium hunting
5. luxurious new red sports
6. ridiculous old Italian
7. beautiful orange Moroccan
8. small round china

Section 20

1. The furniture company <u>soon</u> (declared) bankruptcy.
2. <u>Carefully</u>, Akiro (crossed) the <u>hastily</u> (constructed) bridge.
   [_Carefully_ modifies _crossed_.]
3. <u>Sadly</u>, (Valerie's strike-out ended the game.)
4. The royal caravan made <u>very</u> (slow) progress.
5. <u>Interestingly</u>, (program participants <u>quickly</u> (find) work that is <u>well</u> (paying).)
   [_Interestingly_ modifies the sentence; _quickly_ modifies _find_; _well_ modifies _paying_.]
6. Philippe <u>almost (always)</u> (wins) the office's chess tournament.
   [_Almost_ modifies _always_; _always_ modifies _wins_.]
7. Karen seemed <u>quite</u> (eager) to learn the new security code.
8. (Clive, <u>unbelievably, just</u> (slipped) the letter under the door.)
   [_Unbelievably_ modifies the sentence; _just_ modifies _slipped_.]

Sections 19–20 (1)

1. It was <u>hard</u> work, so he decided to work <u>hard</u>.
   hard work: _hard_ is an adjective
   to work _hard_: _hard_ is an adverb
2. Although she felt <u>happy</u> in her job, she decided, <u>reluctantly</u>, to express <u>very forcefully</u> her <u>growing</u> concern about <u>office</u> politics.
   adjectives: happy, growing, office
   adverbs: reluctantly, very, forcefully
3. The <u>fireplace</u> screen was <u>too hot</u> to touch.
   adjectives: the, fireplace, hot

adverbs: too

4. When <u>the</u> hikers were <u>fully</u> <u>rested</u>, they <u>cheerfully</u> resumed <u>the</u> <u>leisurely</u> pace of their climb.

   adjectives: the, rested, the, leisurely

   adverbs: fully, cheerfully

5. <u>Surely</u> <u>the</u> government can find <u>some</u> way to raise <u>the</u> <u>necessary</u> revenues <u>fairly</u>.

   adjectives: the, some, the, necessary

   adverbs: surely, fairly

Sections 19–20 (2)

1. We enjoyed a **<u>very</u>** good vacation in the Gatineau Hills.
2. She concentrated so **<u>hard</u>** that she got a headache.
3. The promotion usually goes to the **<u>most determined</u>** and **<u>the most skillful</u>** employee.
4. The temperature had risen **<u>considerably</u>** by noon.
5. He preferred to wear his **<u>old blue denim</u>** jacket.
6. Nira isn't writing as **<u>well</u>** as she usually does.
7. Condos are more **<u>costly</u>** this year than they were last.
8. The **<u>slower</u>** you drive, the less fuel you use.
9. He treats his closest friends **<u>worst</u>** of all.
10. Which member of the opposition party is **<u>the most ambitious</u>** politician?

Sections 19–20 (3)

1. **The** buskers **who work in the subway system** sing **exuberantly**.

   who work in the subway system: **adjectival relative clause modifying** *buskers*

   exuberantly: **single-word adverb modifying the verb** *sing*

2. Politicians **opposing tax cuts inevitably** lose **federal** elections.

   opposing tax cuts: **adjectival phrase modifying** *politicians*

   inevitably: **single-word adverb modifying the verb** *lose*

   federal: **single-word adjective modifying the noun** *elections*

3. The goalie **playing during the shoot out** was **suddenly** hit by the puck.

   playing during the shoot out: **adjectival phrase modifying the noun** *goalie*

   suddenly: **single-word adverb modifying the verb** *was hit*

4. Smartphones, **which can perform many functions beyond placing and receiving calls,** are tools.

   which can perform many functions beyond placing and receiving calls: **relative adjectival clause modifying the noun** *smartphones.*

5. There are **countless** lessons **to be learned** in childhood.

   countless: **single-word adjective modifying the noun** *lessons*

   to be learned: **adjectival phrase modifying the noun** *lessons*

Section 21a

1. <u>To succeed in my classes</u> is my most important goal this semester. (noun)
2. Gisella pulled frantically on the dog's leash <u>to keep Rover off the grass.</u> (adverb)

3. The king eventually found a great painter <u>to finish the church fresco.</u> (adjective)
4. Because Jacqueline is so familiar with the drafting software, she refuses <u>to use any other program.</u> (noun)
5. Thinking up some compelling characters is a great way <u>to start writing your novel.</u> (adjective)
6. Our accountant called <u>to apologize.</u> (adverb)
7. Karl is attempting <u>to design the world's largest terrarium.</u> (noun)
8. <u>To reflect recent advancements in the field,</u> the scientist refined her model. (adverb)

Section 21d–e

1. **interest – interesting – interested**

   This novel proved *interesting*.   It was an *interesting* novel.
   The *interested* parties attended the trial.   We stood on the sidelines, *interested*.

   She *is interesting* us in the subject.
   Documentaries *have interested* us for many years now.
   We *should be interested* in the election results.

2. **love – loving – loved**

   She described her parents as *loving*.   She is a *loving* parent.
   The much-*loved* child excelled in school.   *Loved* and protected, she thrived.

   They *will be loving* in their devotion to their elderly parents.
   He *has loved* his partner since the moment they first met.
   A child *must be loved* to be happy.

3. **trouble – troubling – troubled**

   Gun violence seems *troubling*.   The *troubling* data caused controversy.
   He works with *troubled* youth.   *Troubled* by war, we marched for peace.

   The moderator *will be troubling* you to keep your comments brief.
   Unregulated development *has troubled* community leaders for some time now.
   Her behaviour indicates that she *may be troubled* by insomnia.

4. **grow – growing – grown**

   The *growing* city lacks some essential services.
   Grown children often distance themselves from younger siblings.
   He arrived home from his year abroad, *grown* and changed.

   The program *will be growing* significantly because of its larger budget.
   Your baby *has grown* by three inches in the last six months.
   You *will be grown* up the next time you visit.

5. **change – changing – changed**

   Canada has a *changing* economy.
   She is a *changed* woman.
   Changed by her experiences, she found it difficult to resume her routine.

   Technology *has been changing* the ways that we work.
   The government policies *have changed* very little despite widespread protests.
   Can this plan *be changed* before it is implemented?

6. **ride – riding – ridden**

   The *riding* school has just opened.
   This is a well-*ridden* horse.

Ridden twice around the track, the vehicle suddenly broke down.

The jockey *will be riding* a prizewinning horse.
They *have ridden* these paths on their mountain bikes.
That horse *should* not *be ridden* by inexperienced children.

7. **excite – exciting – excited**

The election race became *exciting*.
It became an *exciting* election race.
The reporter seemed *excited* and breathless.
Excited and breathless, the reporter went on the air with her story.

The actor *will be exciting* the audience with his dazzling swordplay.
The clown *has excited* that audience of children with his pratfalls.
A dedicated scientist *can be excited* by the sight of a test tube.

8. **dry – drying – dried**

The *drying* canvas stood on the artist's easel.
Dried fruits are a popular item sold at this shop.
Dried out, the parched landscape showed the effects of the drought.

After swimming in the ocean, we *were drying* out on the beach.
Have you *been drying* your wet hair in the warm spring sunshine?
The wet paint *can be dried* with a high-powered fan.

9. **bake – baking – baked**

This recipe calls for the use of *baking* powder.
Baked goods are often high in carbohydrates.
Baked and packaged, the cupcakes were offered for sale.

She *is baking* her own wedding cake.
The wedding cake *had been baked* a week before it was iced.
You *can bake* in the desert sun if you're not careful.

Section 21 (1)

1. Krystoff thoroughly enjoys <u>rowing in the summer</u>. (gerund—noun, direct object)
2. Everyone at the dojo wanted <u>to go to the martial arts competition</u>. (infinitive—noun, direct object)
3. <u>Purposely distracting the other players</u> is not fair. (gerund—noun, subject)
4. This poem, <u>neatly encapsulating James Reaney's work</u>, appears in his last collection. (participle—adjective modifying *poem*)
5. Carolyn researches cognitive psychology <u>to understand language better</u>. (infinitive—adverb modifying *researches*)
6. The audience stared at the images <u>projected on the screen</u>. (participle—adjective modifying *images*)
7. <u>Applying quantitative research methods to this problem</u> will result in a much different conclusion. (gerund—noun, subject)
8. Eventually Lyuba gained the confidence <u>to write longer papers that were also more persuasive</u>. (infinitive—adjective modifying *confidence*).
9. The poll found the majority of voters <u>resisting the idea of changes to the education system</u>. (participle—adjective modifying *voters*)
10. The guy <u>asking all of those questions</u> must be an upper-year student. (participle—adjective

modifying *the guy*)

Section 21 (2)

1. <u>Coming</u> as he did from the Prairies, he found the coastal scenery <u>to be stunning</u>.
   coming – present participle   **stunning – present participle**
   to be – infinitive
2. She wanted <u>to snowboard</u>, and <u>learning</u> was easier than she had expected.
   to snowboard – infinitive   **learning – gerund**
3. <u>Trying to study</u> hard on an empty stomach is usually not very <u>rewarding</u>.
   trying – gerund   **rewarding – present participle**
   to study – infinitive
4. The dinner was certain <u>to last</u> until midnight, <u>permitting</u> everyone <u>to eat</u> and <u>drink</u> too much.
   to last – infinitive   **to eat – infinitive**
   permitting – present participle   **(to) drink – infinitive**
5. <u>Sent</u> as she had <u>been</u> from one office to another, Cindy was <u>tired</u> of <u>running</u> back and forth and up and down; she was <u>resolved</u> <u>to go</u> straight to the top.
   sent – past participle   **running – gerund**
   been – past participle   **resolved – past participle**
   tired – past participle   **to go – infinitive**

Section 21 (3)

A.
1. **to read**
   noun: To read is educational. (subject)
             I love to read. (object)
             One path to intellectual enlightenment is to read. (predicate noun)
   adjective: I am looking for a good book to read.
   adverb: You require patience in order to read.
   noun phrase: To read, curled up in a big stuffed chair, is one of my favourite pastimes.
2. **to listen**
   noun: To listen is essential. (subject)
             You need to listen. (object)
             One part of learning is to read. (predicate noun)
   adjective: I am looking for a good spot to listen.
   adverb: You are required to stay awake in order to listen.
   noun phrase: To listen, silent and thoughtful, is one of his most impressive gifts.
3. **to laugh**
   noun: To laugh is essential to good health. (subject)
             I love to laugh. (object)
             One way to express yourself is to laugh. (predicate noun)
   adjective: I want to laugh.
   adverb: You require a good sense of humour in order to laugh.
   noun phrase: To laugh, head back and eyes alight with mischief, is one of the important
             requirements of this role.

B.
1. The **singing** chef prepared three entrees at once. (present participle modifying the subject *chef*)

2. She chided the **jaded** reporter. (past participle modifying the direct object *reporter*)
3. We gave the **waiting** children a box of building blocks. (present participle modifying the indirect object *children*)
4. The purpose of **debating** clubs is to practise oral argument. (present participle modifying the *clubs*, the object of the preposition *of*)
5. This piece of music is an **undoubted** masterpiece. (past participle modifying the predicate noun *masterpiece*)
6. We declared the candidate an **emerging** leader. (present participle modifying the objective complement *leader*)
7. Madeleine Thein, an **accomplished** novelist, has also published short stories and a picture book for children. (past participle modifying the appositive noun *novelist*)
8. The doctor treated the **coughing** patient. (present participle modifying the direct object *patient*)
9. The newspaper article has been reprinted in this **celebrated** book. (past participle modifying *book*, the object of the preposition *in*)
10. The **seasoned** broadcaster conducted the interview with the new prime minister. (past participle modifying the subject *broadcaster*)

Section 21 (4)

1. Her most important goal was **to graduate**.
2. Hubert went to the Chinese restaurant **to eat**.
3. **Thinking tuition is too high**, some students protested today.
4. Juvenile diabetes is a disease **affecting many Canadian children**.
5. These days, some of my friends always talk about **getting married**.
6. The test has five questions you need **to answer**.
7. **Laughing**, Paul gave his answer.
8. **Painting** our house was more work than we thought.

Section 21 (5)

1. Sometimes the best part of a vacation is **planning it**.
2. Earning the respect of children is something **to be proud of**.
3. **Feeling foolish**, they decided to leave early.
4. **Winning the contest** came as something of a shock to her.
5. The bank manager **wearing the colourful wig** started doing the samba.

Section 21 (6)

1. Remember **to be** at the computer lab by 3:30.
2. The quarterback's problem was **to decide** what play **to use** next.
3. My charismatic cousin gestured to us **to follow** him into the restaurant.
4. The time **to worry** about is the hour before the race.
5. After the motorbike came to a grinding halt, Abigail pondered what **to do** next.

Section 21 (7)

1. **The toddler being very sleepy**, her father carried her upstairs to her bedroom.

2. **Nose running and eyes watering**, he sat down, hoping he had chopped enough onions.
3. **Lights flickering and computer groaning**, the 100-page report disappeared from the screen.
4. **The day breezy yet warm**, they decided to take their golden retriever for a walk in Hyde Park.
5. **Extra money being hard to come by**, he was forced to curtail his marathon shopping trips to New York City.

Section 21 (8)

1. Its leaves wilted, the fern appeared to be dying.
2. Tonya watched her daughter dance on stage, her face beaming with happiness.
3. His head throbbing, his hands shaking, Harman didn't even know where he was.
4. On the left side of the apartment was the entrance, the door boarded up.
5. Having worked with Gianna for ten years, Phil could not imagine running the company without her.
6. Colby's suspicions having been confirmed, he walked out without a word.
7. Emma saw the dog, its tail wagging, come over the hilltop.
8. Their trip nearly finished, Jahir and Olivia decided to spend their last day in Stanley Park.

Sections 22a–c (1)

1. <u>Throughout</u> our visit <u>to</u> the territory's capital, we made constant excursions <u>beyond</u> the outskirts <u>of</u> Whitehorse.
2. Clarissa is skilled <u>at</u> math.
3. While I completed the assignment, Sarah checked her email <u>on</u> the laptop.
4. <u>Before</u> you leave, please place the dirty dishes <u>in</u> the kitchen <u>onto</u> the counter <u>beside</u> the sink.
5. We brought all the files <u>concerning</u> the case <u>except</u> the ones <u>with</u> the records <u>from</u> January.
6. Finnegan is meeting us <u>after</u> class.
7. The professor requested that everyone who fell asleep <u>during</u> the film stay behind <u>after</u> class.
8. Daniel is standing near the cubicle <u>opposite</u> the photocopier.
9. Aziz made several calls <u>regarding</u> the business deal.
10. <u>Beneath</u> the roads and buildings lies a network <u>of</u> sewers, <u>without</u> which the city could not exist.

Section 22a–c (2)

1. Josh went <u>into town</u> to buy some back bacon <u>for his breakfast</u>.
   into town – adverbial   **for his breakfast – adjectival**
2. There stood the famous pianist <u>of about thirty</u>, <u>in the hot sunshine</u>, wearing a heavy jacket <u>with the collar</u> turned up.
   of about thirty – adjectival   **with the collar – adjectival**
   in the hot sunshine – adverbial
3. <u>In the morning</u> the president called her assistant <u>on the telephone</u> and told her to come <u>to the office</u> <u>without delay</u>.

in the morning – adverbial	to the office – adverbial
on the telephone – adverbial	without delay – adverbial

4. The bulk <u>of the presents</u> was sent ahead <u>in trunks</u>.

of the presents – adjectival	**in trunks – adverbial**

5. The Siamese cat looked <u>under the table</u> <u>for the ball</u> <u>of yarn</u> that had fallen <u>from the chair</u>.

under the table – adverbial	**of yarn – adjectival**
for the ball – adverbial	**from the chair – adverbial**

Section 22a–c (3)

A. REDUCING CLAUSES TO PREPOSITIONAL PHRASES

1. **With enough stamina**, you can take part in the triathlon.
2. **Because of her great self-confidence**, she entered every race.
3. Students **with part-time jobs** must budget their time carefully.
4. We need **the** advice **of a grandmother**.
5. The **best** time **to eat** is three hours before you go to sleep.

B. REDUCING CLAUSES TO PREPOSITIONAL PHRASES USING GERUNDS

1. **After running only half a block**, I felt exhausted.
2. **Despite having trained rigorously**, Petra didn't get past the preliminaries.
3. You can't hope to understand **without attending all the classes**.
4. **After checking the luggage carefully**, they found nothing but a pair of toe nail clippers. [or, **Upon checking the luggage carefully**, . . .]
5. He deserves some credit **for trying so hard**.

C. GETTING RID OF EXCESSIVE PREPOSITIONAL PHRASES

1. Sarah reached the mountaintop first when she used several trails unknown to her competitors in the race celebrating the centennial of the province's entering confederation. (9 prepositional phrases reduced to 3)
2. Most people attending the meeting felt that the committee chair spoke stridently and lengthily on topics he did not fully understand. (7 prepositional phrases reduced to 1)
3. The irritated ghost who haunted the old house stood atop the staircase and shouted, 'Get away from the door—and hurry!' (6 prepositional phrases reduced to 1)
4. The highly respected modern historian has some odd ideas about how the First World War, which started in early August 1914 and had such devastating consequences for European and other nations, began. (8 prepositional phrases reduced to 3)
5. Economists predict rising and falling interest rates quite accurately, but principally within three or four week periods; even then, you should view their forecasts cautiously or skeptically. (10 prepositional phrases reduced to 1)

Section 23a

1. Uma was late for the meeting, **but** she had a good excuse.
2. There is only one solution to this problem, **and** I know what it is.
3. No one likes noise pollution, **yet (but)** some people insist that we have to live with it.
4. Her brother is not cynical, **nor** is he insensitive.
5. We were puzzled by the professor's humorous comments, **for** we had expected her to speak seriously on the subject.

6. The tuba solo came as a surprise, **for** Tomas and Uli were expecting an organ concerto.
7. She had two choices: she could fasten the component with rivets, **or** she could create a new design.
8. Theoretical developments are not neatly insulated from one another, **nor** are they arranged in neat phases.

Section 23c (1)

(1) *when he was only eight*: acting as an adverb modifying the verb *decided*; *(that) he wanted to be a marine biologist*: acting as a noun clause; direct object of the verb *decided*

(2) *where his family stayed every summer*: acting as an adjective modifying the noun *cabin*

(3) *as he grew older*: acting as an adverb modifying the verb *discovered*; *that in order to become a marine biologist*: noun clause; direct object of the verb *discovered*; *that seemed far removed from ocean life*: acting as an adjective modifying the noun *subjects*

(4) *whenever he worked on his math, statistics, or computer problems in stuffy rooms*: acting as an adverb modifying the verb *kept* (longing)

(5) *That he became a successful field scientist and expert on the microorganisms found in tide pools*: noun clause acting as the subject of *is*

(6) *what most people don't know*: noun clause; subject of the verb *is*; *that when Selwyn became a full professor, he didn't need to worry about doing analysis anymore*: noun clause; subjective complement of the verb *is*; *when Selwyn became a full professor*: acting as an adverb modifying the verb *didn't need*; *because he had graduate students*: acting as an adverb modifying the verb *didn't need to worry*; *who enjoyed working with numbers*: acting as an adjective modifying the noun *students*; *who derived satisfaction from developing new approaches to data analysis*: acting as an adjective modifying the noun *students*

(7) *while they crunched numbers*: acting as an adverb modifying the verb *puttered*

Section 23c (2)

1. Ida is training very hard because she wants to go to the olympics.
2. They stopped for lunch after they went to the museum.
3. We included an extra key in case you lose the other one.
4. Corporations will pollute the oceans unless we create stronger government regulations.
5. If you haven't brought your registration, you will have to wait in line.
6. Annie thinks she should work on commission whereas her boss thinks Annie should be paid hourly.
7. Until Karen arrived, Harold waited.
8. The cottage where we brought the hammocks didn't have any trees.

Section 23c (3)

1. *As the art gallery won't open until next week*, the leak in the roof hasn't been repaired yet.
2. *As long as (While) Canada's gun laws are still stricter than those in the United States*, we should defend this.
3. *Because some students may not have paid all their fees*, they would not yet be considered officially registered.
4. You should master the simple sentence *before you work on rhyming couplets*.
5. *Because (After) the children ate most of their Halloween candy*, they were bouncing off the

walls.

Section 23 (1)

(1) Shuter <u>and</u> Victoria (coordinating)

(2) poignancy, <u>for</u> he (coordinating)

(3) costly, <u>but</u> he (coordinating); Carnegie Hall <u>or</u> London's (coordinating)

(4) <u>After</u> construction (subordinating)

(5) the hall has <u>not only</u> presented thousands of concerts, <u>but also</u> hosted (correlative); tournaments, <u>and</u> even typing (coordinating)

(6) Maria Callas, <u>and</u> Bob Marley (coordinating)

(7) performers <u>whenever</u> they stop (subordinating).

Sections 23 (2)

1. **Example:** She lead the team not only in assists but also in goals.
2. **Example:** Winter started late this year, and spring started early.
3. **Example:** *Hamlet* could have been written in 1601 or 1602.
4. **Example:** The crowd applauded when the ballerinas returned to the stage.
5. **Example:** Either Hiroto will make you sashimi or Teru will make you steak.
6. **Example:** The Rosetta stone is an amazing object, but who owns it?
7. **Example:** The carnival ended before the Ferris wheel broke down.
8. **Example:** You enrolled in physics, so you don't have to enrol in math.
9. **Example:** Both the judges and the other divers were impressed.
10. **Example:** The turtle swam across the aquarium, and the biologist marked it in her records.

Sections 13–24

1. The [article] lazy [adjective] boatman [noun] was [verb] sleeping [gerund (adjective)], so [conjunction] she [personal pronoun] boldly [adverb] crossed [verb] the [article] river [noun] herself [intensive pronoun].

2. Since [subordinating conjunction] she [personal pronoun] became [verb] a [article] manager [noun], Jelina [noun] hardly [adverb] talks [verb] to [preposition] us [personal pronoun] anymore [adverb].

3. Alas [interjection], I [pronoun] cannot [modal auxiliary verb] present [main verb] my [pronoun] paper [noun] in [preposition] class [noun] this [adjective] Saturday [noun].

4. Deadly [adjective] wildfires [noun] devastate [verb] the [pronoun] Australian [adjective] countryside [noun].

5. We [pronoun] knew [verb] each other [reflexive pronoun] before [adverb] the [article] war [noun], but [subordinating conjunction] we [personal pronoun] never [adverb] spoke [verb].

6. Sabastian [noun] recited [verb] his [possessive adjective] litany [noun] of [preposition] worsening [adjective] facts [noun] and [conjunction] figures [noun], including [preposition] the [article] latest [adjective] hunger [predicative noun] statistics [noun].

7. A [article] large [adjective] raccoon [noun] quietly [adverb] invaded [verb] the [article] cottage [noun] because [subordinating conjunction] it [pronoun] sensed [verb] food [noun] inside [adjective].

8.   Whoever [relative pronoun] left [verb] these [adjective] potato [predicative noun] chips [noun] on [preposition] the [article] floor [noun] will [auxiliary verb] suffer [verb] serious [adjective] consequences [noun] when [adverb] I [personal pronoun] find [verb] him [personal pronoun].

9.   They [personal pronoun] just [adverb] figured [verb] that [subordinating conjunction] because [subordinating conjunction] he [pronoun] was [verb] from [preposition] another [adjective] country [noun] hockey [noun] would [auxiliary verb] be [verb] foreign [adjective] to [preposition] him [personal pronoun].

10.   We [personal pronoun] travelled [verb] on [preposition] large [adjective] boats [noun] for [preposition] years [noun], but [coordinating conjunction] travelling [gerund (noun)] on [preposition] a [article] train [noun] is [verb] a [article] completely [adverb] new [adjective] experience [noun] to [preposition] my [possessive adjective] brother [noun] and [conjunction] me [personal pronoun].

Review exercises: Part III

A. RECOGNIZING PARTS OF SPEECH

1. **The** [article, modifying the noun *skyline*] **skyline** [noun, subject of *provides*] **of** [preposition] **modern** [adjective, modifying *Toronto*] **Toronto** [noun, object of the preposition *of*] **provides** [verb] **a** [article, modifying the noun *example*] **striking** [adjective modifying the noun *example*] **example** [noun, direct object of *provides*] **of** [preposition] **what** [relative pronoun, subordinate conjunction] **modern** [adjective modifying the noun *architecture*] **architecture** [noun, object of the preposition *of*] **can** [modal auxiliary verb] **do** [main verb] **to** [preposition (part of the infinitive verb *to distinguish*)] **distinguish** [verbal (infinitive verb form)] **a** [article modifying the noun *city*] **major** [adjective modifying the noun *city*] **city** [noun]. **(The sentence is declarative and complex.)**

2. **Waiter** [noun], **there's** [*there* (expletive) + *is* (linking verb)] **a** [article, modifying the noun *fly*] **fly** [noun, subjective complement of the verb *is*] **doing** [present participle] **the** [article, modifying the noun *crawl*] **back** [adjective modifying the noun *crawl*] **crawl** [noun, object of the verbal *doing*] **in** [preposition] **my** [possessive adjective, modifying the noun *soup*] **soup** [noun, object of the preposition *in*]! **(The sentence is exclamatory and simple.)**

3. **Well** [interjection], **to** [preposition, marking the infinitive verb *tell*] **tell** [verb in its infinitive form] **the** [article, modifying the noun *truth*] **truth** [noun, object of the infinitive *to tell*] **I** [pronoun, subject of the verb *did not have*] **just** [adverb, modifying the verb *did not have*] **did** [modal auxiliary verb] **not** [adverb, modifying the verb *did have*] **have** [main verb] **the** [article, modifying the noun *patience*] **necessary** [adjective, modifying the noun *patience*] **patience** [noun, direct object of *did not have*]! **(The sentence is exclamatory and simple.)**

4. **Why** [interrogative adverb] **should** [modal auxiliary verb] **anyone** [indefinite pronoun] **be** [main verb] **unhappy** [predicate adjective, modifying the pronoun *anyone*] **about** [preposition] **paying** [gerund, object of the preposition *about*] **a** [article, modifying the noun *tax*] **fair** [adjective, modifying the noun *tax*] **tax** [noun, object of the gerund *paying*]? **(The sentence is interrogative and simple.)**

5. **Neither** [correlative conjunction] **the** [article, modifying the noun *captain*] **captain** [noun, subject of *could be blamed*] **nor** [correlative conjunction] **the** [article, modifying the noun *crew*] **crew** [noun, subject of *could be blamed*] **could** [modal auxiliary verb] **be** [auxiliary verb] **blamed** [main verb, past participle form] **for** [preposition] **the** [article, modifying the noun *accident*] **terribly** [adverb, modifying the adjective *costly*] **costly** [adjective, modifying the noun *accident*] **ferry** [adjective, modifying the noun *accident*] **accident** [noun, object of the preposition *for*]. **(The sentence is declarative and simple.)**

6. **The** (article, modifying the noun *business*) **elevator** [adjective, modifying the noun *business*] **business** [noun, subject of the verb *has been said*] **has** [auxiliary verb] **been** [auxiliary verb, past participle form] **said** [main verb, past participle form] **to** [preposition, introducing the infinitive verb *have*] **have** [infinitive verb form] **its** [possessive adjective, modifying *ups* and *downs*] **ups** [noun, direct object of the infinitive verb *to have*] **and** [coordinating conjunction] **downs** [noun, direct object of the infinitive verb *to have*]. **(The sentence is declarative and simple.)**

7. **Don** [noun of direct address], **please** [interjection] **put** [verb] **back** [adverb, particle in the two-part verb *put back*] **the** [article, modifying the noun *cake*] **chocolate** [adjective, modifying the noun *cake*] **cake** [noun, direct object of the verb *put (back)*]. **(The sentence is imperative and simple.)**

8. **While** [adverb] **abroad** [adverb], **I** [personal pronoun, subject of the verb *learned*] **learned** [verb] **to** [preposition, introducing the infinitive verb *make*] **manage** [verb, infinitive form] **with** [preposition] **only** [adverb, modifying the adjective *three*] **three** [adjective, modifying

the noun suitcases] **large** [adjective, modifying the noun *suitcases*] **suitcases** [noun, object of the preposition *with*] **and** [coordinating conjunction] **one** [adjective, modifying the noun *chauffeur*] **full-time** [adjective, modifying the noun *chauffeur*] **chauffeur** [noun, object of the preposition *with*]. **(The sentence is declarative and simple.)**

9. **In** [preposition] **a** [article, modifying the noun *seconds*] **few** [adjective, modifying the noun *seconds*] **seconds** [noun, object of the preposition *in*], **the** [article, modifying the noun *computer*] **computer** [noun, subject of the verb *told*] **told** [verb] **us** [personal pronoun, indirect object of the verb *told*] **much** [adjective, modifying the noun *more*] **more** [noun] **than** [conjunction] **we** [personal pronoun, subject of the verb *needed*] **needed** [verb] **to** [preposition, introducing the infinitive verb *know*] **know** [verb in infinitive form]. **(The sentence is declarative and complex.)**

10. **Help** [verb]! **(The sentence is exclamatory and simple.)**

B. USING DIFFERENT PARTS OF SPEECH

shed	They shed their parkas in the midday sunshine. (verb)
	You'll find the gardening tools in the shed. (noun)
best	This book is the best source on the topic of workplace stress. (adjective)
	Our aim is to best the opposing team in our defensive performance. (verb)
left	She made a left turn at the wrong traffic light. (adjective)
	We left the party after the guest of honour made his speech. (verb)
plant	The company moved its new plant from Hamilton to Peterborough. (noun)
	The team decided to plant the flag at the North Pole. (verb)
before	Before the first intermission, members of the audience fell asleep. (preposition)
	The candidates shook hands before they began the debate. (subordinate conjunction)
still	We still aim to spend the summer in the mountains. (adverb)
	The still life hanging in the gallery is the object of a bidding war. (adjective)
train	The train wound its way across the prairie. (noun)
	These athletes train at the aquatic centre every morning. (verb)
cover	The cover image is vivid and disturbing. (adjective)
	The chef will cover the dish with a spicy sauce. (verb)
	What is on the cover of the magazine this month? (noun)
wrong	Without a map, we were bound to take a wrong turn on our journey. (adjective)
	We exhausted ourselves in debating the right and the wrong of the issue. (noun)
last	How long will this blizzard last? (verb)
	The students caught the last bus to Mont-Tremblant. (adjective)
round	As we round the corner, we will see the monument. (verb)
	The sixth round of the competition ended in a tie. (noun)
	The square peg will not fit in the round hole. (adjective)
set	I won the second set, but I lost the match to a superior tennis player. (noun)
	Please set the table when you have a moment. (verb)
rose	The rose is a symbol of love and beauty. (noun)
	The defendant rose to hear the jury's verdict. (verb)
	She is knitting a rose scarf. (adjective)
cross	Do they plan to cross the border at the Peace Arch Crossing? (verb)
	When the legislators disagree, they are at cross purposes. (adjectives)
	The cross is an important symbol of Christianity. (noun)
near	The children played near the soccer field. (preposition)
	We travelled near and far. (adverb)

Part IV
Writing Effective Sentences

Lengthening sentences
pp. 201–202

Redraft the following paragraph to practise creating longer sentences.

Whitewater rafting is an outdoor activity. It is perfect for people who want an adventure. Several participants get into a boat. They navigate down a river. These rivers have different degrees of rough water. Many people think it is exciting. Other people think it is too dangerous. Experienced guides make the difference. An average guide will show you how to be safe. The best guides also teach you safety. However, they also make sure the experience is exciting.

Shortening sentences
p. 202

Redraft the following paragraph to practise creating shorter sentences.

The views of environmentalists and the tourism industry frequently clash over the use of natural areas because environmentalists know the negative effects an increased human presence can have on remote areas, and they strive to preserve the ecological integrity of these areas. Conversely, the tourism industry points to the often limited economic opportunities that exist in remote areas, and they frequently argue that successful tourism can be an excellent revenue source for the remote communities. Finding compromise will not be easy, but it is possible.

Sentence variety

pp. 202–204

Redraft the following paragraph to practise creating variety by using different types of sentences.

Ideally, our project will introduce several different learning styles. Certainly, you will already know one or two of these styles. Fortunately, our project will describe the rest of these styles. We start our project with brief outlines of the most familiar styles because these are easy to understand. We continue our project with the less familiar styles because these styles are more abstract. We conclude our project with a list of practical applications because all of these styles are useful for aspiring teachers.

Sentence length, variety, and emphasis

pp. 201–210

Below are four paragraphs from draft versions of student essays. For practice, revise each one to improve the effectiveness of sentence length, variety, and emphasis. Try not to change the basic sense in any important way, but make whatever changes will make the paragraphs effective.

1. My father drove up to the campsite and chose an empty spot close to the lake, up against the thickly covered mountainside. We had just unpacked our equipment and set up our tent when an elderly man walked up our path. He introduced himself and told us that he was camped farther up the mountain, about a hundred yards away. He told us that only an hour before, as he walked toward his campsite, he saw a huge black bear running away from it. He said he then drew closer and saw that his tent was knocked down and his food scattered all over the ground. He suggested that we might want to move our camp to a safer place, not so close to this bear's haunts.

2. The sky promised hot and sunny weather as we quickly finished closing side-pockets and adjusting straps on our packs in preparation for our hike up Black Tusk, which is in Garibaldi Park, a hike which was to be on a trail I had never seen before and which I therefore had been looking forward to with great enthusiasm. And that's what I felt as we set off in the early morning light on the first leg of the journey which would take us to the top in a few hours.

3. The way time passes can be odd. The mind's sense of time can be changed. I remember an experience which will illustrate this. It happened when I was nine. I rode my bike in front of a car and got hit. I don't remember much about this experience. However, a few details do come to mind. These include the way the car's brakes sounded suddenly from my right. I never even saw the car that hit me. And I remember flying through the air. It was a peculiar feeling. The ground seemed to come up slowly as I floated along. Time seemed almost to have stopped. But then I hit the ground. And then time speeded up. A neighbour ran up and asked if I was all right. My parents pulled our car up. They carefully put me in it. And all of a sudden I was at the hospital, it seemed. It all must have taken twenty or thirty minutes. To me it seemed that only a minute or two had passed since I had hit the ground.

4. It's not so difficult to repot a houseplant, although many plant owners procrastinate about doing this because they think it's too messy and time-consuming, when actually repotting takes very little time and effort if you follow a simple set of instructions such as I'm about to give you. And you'll find that when you've done the repotting both you and your plant will benefit from the process because the plant will then be able to receive fresh minerals and oxygen from the new soil which will make it grow into a healthier plant that will give you increased pleasure and enjoyment.

Correcting sentence fragments

p. 214

Identify and correct the fragments in the following exercises. Place a check mark beside any that do not require a correction.

Example: Municipalities across the province have planned new parks. With construction already underway in North Battleford, Estevan, Swift Current, Moose Jaw, and Yorkton.

Municipalities across the province have planned new parks. Construction is already underway in North Battleford, Estevan, Swift Current, Moose Jaw, and Yorkton.

1. Even when we account for fluctuations in the experiment's key variables. We obtain similar results.

2. Sit down! They will be here shortly.

3. The young politician earnestly applied herself to her first assignment. A municipal council subcommittee responsible for road sign replacement.

4. Solar panels offer several advantages. Usable almost anywhere, quiet, non-polluting, and mechanically reliable compared with many other renewable sources.

5. We finally found the young boy. Hungry, dirty, and crying.

6. Clarissa having purchased the flowers herself. The maid continued sleeping.

7. The man stood in front of the stadium. Asking all who passed by if they needed tickets for the game.

8. To present the residents with a greater range of services. The town council commissioned an addition to the community centre.

9. Bathurst, Campbellton, Edmunston, Fredericton, and Miramichi. All of these cities have courthouses.

10. For many cultural anthropologists. Ethnographic fieldwork is the quintessential anthropological experience.

Correcting sentence fragments

p. 214

Identify and correct the sentence fragments in the following paragraph.

(1) We used a book to identify the unusual new bird in the field behind our house. (2) We discovered it was a spruce grouse. (3) A medium-sized grouse with a long black tail with brown at the end. (4) We weren't sure why it chose the field. (5) There being little food nearby and no suitable undergrowth for nesting. (6) The bird arrived at the end of fall. (7) We kept an eye on it through the entire winter. (8) Watching it scratch out an existence. (9) Our bird was constantly foraging. (10) For what, I am not sure. (11) It mostly ate the needles from the nearby conifer trees. (12) We usually let nature take its course. (13) Because we live in a rural area. (14) And although we don't like to disturb nature, we eventually put out some seeds for the bird to eat. (15) Our bird appearing too cold and hungry not to leave it something. (16) The next day it disappeared. (17) Which is why we decided never to feed the birds in the field again.

Correcting misplaced modifiers
pp. 216–218

Identify and correct the misplaced modifiers in the following sentences.

1. The department needed funds in order to teach the students badly.

2. The duettists left the stage that inspired a standing ovation.

3. If you want to help, only be sure to donate to the victims of the floods through registered charities.

4. Eugene called me from the beach and asked me if I wanted to go surfing on his phone.

5. Covered in her article, Elaina posted links to all of the key topics.

6. Ravi was preparing some dishes for his friends that weren't so spicy.

7. Already having read the magazines in the waiting room, Sui-Jei stared simply at the ceiling.

8. The thief was found in the park that stole the treasure.

9. The skateboarder was excited to get to the skatepark with new green shoes.

10. My lemonade stand was so successful this weekend that I nearly made $150.

Correcting misplaced modifiers

pp. 216–218

Revise the following sentences to eliminate awkwardness resulting from misplaced modifiers.

1. They discussed booking a trip around the world for two days but decided against it.

2. I pledged to always listen to my children when I became a parent.

3. She decided that on this day she would skip dinner entirely in the morning.

4. I could see my grandmother coming through the window.

5. Our submissions were accepted if they were postmarked only by midnight.

6. A piano stood in the centre of the stage with its outline only visible to the audience in the darkness.

7. The newspaper only published three letters to the editor yesterday.

8. It merely seemed a few days before he returned from his journey to Nepal.

Correcting dangling modifiers

pp. 218–222

Identify the dangling modifier and suggest a correction. Place a check mark beside any that do not require a correction.

1. Before turning on the electricity, her wiring diagram was inspected.

2. By performing with a Quebecois group, his popularity surged.

3. While resting at the café with our drinks, a flock of starlings settled on the oak tree.

4. To fully appreciate Carson's poetry, it helps to be familiar with classical literature.

5. When six years old, my grandmother opened my eyes to the joys of crochet.

6. As a leading paleontologist, one of the professor's areas of expertise is skeletal reconstruction.

7. To improve your deking, you must practice.

8. Texting often, the conversation between my boyfriend and me is continuous.

9. Unless the leaves are raked, you will have to stay home and miss football practice.

10. After finishing the planning, the writing is easy.

Correcting dangling modifiers

pp. 218–222

Revise the following sentences to eliminate dangling modifiers.

1. Sitting quiet and fascinated, the hyperactive hummingbird was gazed at by the baby in her playpen.

2. By using first-person narration, readers are led by the author to wonder about the reliability of the story.

3. In order to cook, one must be creative, thereby being adept at substituting one ingredient for another.

4. Looked at in this light, one has to find Hamlet very much like other people.

5. Réaumur introduced the idea of testing small sample rods and then studying their structure when fractured.

6. Being the youngest member of the community, it is harder for me to convince the elders of my experience.

7. When not going to school or working, my activities range from playing tennis to surfing the Internet.

8. By using this style it added more tension to the dialogue.

9. The colonel began to send groups of reinforcements to the weakened position only to be ambushed in the mountain passes.

10. Whispering in the darkened theatre, our popcorn spilled onto the floor.

Review of common sentence errors
pp. 214–222

Identify and revise all fragments, comma splice errors, run-on sentences, and misplaced or dangling modifiers in the following paragraphs.

(1) Although some people assume lobsters are fished everywhere in the Maritimes, lobsters mostly live in a few areas off the east coast. (2) Preferring to live in waters with an abundance of rocks and seaweed, most of the lobster fishing in Canada takes place in the ocean waters in the Gulf of the St. Lawrence or southwest Nova Scotia. (3) In fact, weighing in at just over 20 kilograms, a Nova Scotia fisherman boasts catching the largest lobster on record. (4) Lobsters are Canada's most valuable seafood export, Canada ships these crustaceans around the world to fifty-nine countries. (5) Reports estimate their export value to the Canadian economy at nearly one billion dollars they are the primary source of income in many maritime communities.

(6) As with many other natural resources, the lobster fishery is in danger of being exploited unsustainably. (7) In fact, some argue that it is already being overused, however, all levels of both government and the people who fish lobster are making efforts to use the resource responsibly. (8) Minimum shell sizes are set so that lobsters in their prime breeding years are not removed from the ocean. (9) As well as any female lobsters carrying eggs. (10) In addition to rules about acceptable lobster size, the size and number of traps is limited. (11) Traps must be constructed so that smaller lobsters are allowed to escape and they must be made of biodegradable materials so that lobsters aren't trapped if the trap gets lost. (12) We will only be able to measure the success of these efforts in future years.

With information from Fisheries and Oceans Canada, 2013. Web. 7 Jan 2013. http://www.dfo-mpo.gc.ca/index-eng.htm

Correcting mixed constructions

pp. 222–223

Revise the following sentences to eliminate mixed constructions.

1. The reason for the decrease in tourism was due to the fear of terrorism.

2. Soccer happens to be a sport is very popular in Brazil.

3. I found that the children's literature website to be very useful.

4. The new styles were popular with both men or women alike.

5. Since, for most of us, our earliest recollections are mere fragments of things that made up our childhoods, we therefore must rely on the objects or ideas around us to trigger the past.

6. Just because people like to watch reality television programs is not a sign of a decadent society.

Correcting mixed constructions

pp. 222–223

Revise the following sentences to eliminate mixed constructions.

1. Patients who have a low white blood cell count can mean something is seriously wrong.

2. Although she is involved in the communist party doesn't mean she hates democracy.

3. Rover is a rambunctious spaniel, who, as he grows older, his charm grows as well.

4. With the momentum being increased, it will alter the trajectory.

5. True wisdom is when you admit you know nothing.

6. An electric barrier, the town council's controversial new plan, was drafted by the mayor.

7. The reason the artists are joining the protest because of the cuts to the papier mâché budget.

8. By observing the results of the study has given us insight into consumer behaviour

Improving alignment
pp. 223–224

Revise the following sentences to remove illogical or incongruous alignment.

1. The nearly two hours of congratulatory of speeches at convocation went on for far too long.

2. The complicated device was an example of a determined group effort.

3. Even new psychological theories cannot understand all learning disabilities.

4. Waiting lists for a kidney transplant can take months, even years.

5. Her restraint failed to satisfy the teacher.

6. Alcohol is an escape from reality for some people.

7. Many of the forty-six defendants found guilty in the month of July resulted from what the legal system calls "driving under the influence."

8. Fortunately, the news that Meredith was anxiously expecting came true.

9. This photocopier prefers to be fed paper one sheet at a time.

10. Setting the temperature in our office, once adjusted by hand, is now controlled electronically.

Improving alignment

pp. 223–224

Revise the following sentences to remove illogical or incongruous alignment.

1. I decided not to buy it, for the price was too expensive.

2. Even religious principles were being enlightened during this period.

3. It is clear that this general conception of his ability is greatly underestimated.

4. The only source of light in the house came through the windows.

5. Its shape is a rectangle about three times as long as it is wide.

6. The poem expresses the meaningless and useless achievements of war.

7. The character of the speaker in the poem seems euphoric and energetic.

8. The need for such great effort on the part of the reader represents serious weakness in the writing.

9. Life and death was a constant idea in the back of the pioneers' minds.

10. She started university at a very young age.

Eliminating shifts

pp. 225–226

Revise the following sentences to eliminate shifts.

1. Leslie had been training for months before the rugby coach invites her to try out for the team.

2. Her letter said that years ago the farmers had wanted to build a facility for converting manure into saleable methane, but financial woes make that impossible.

3. I took the bus to the museum and see Belinda walking out with Stuart.

4. A person who wants to learn how to play piano must be dedicated because you have to practice every day.

5. When the firefighters arrived at the burning building, the roof could be seen erupting into flames.

6. Read the first chapter of the book, and you should answer each of the questions provided.

7. If a person doesn't follow a healthy diet, you can suffer a stroke or heart attack.

8. Although some people see the value in these regulations, there are others who do not.

9. When you write back, please let me know if there are any questions.

10. We tool and die makers take pride in our trade, and our projects are always completed on schedule.

Correcting faulty parallelism
pp. 227–230

Revise the following sentences in order to repair faulty parallelism.

1. When plotting other ships on the map, you should consider how fast they are travelling, what direction they are travelling, and their location.

2. Our new application is designed for retrieving data, creating files, and the compression of information.

3. Gustaff showed the professor that his funding was sufficient and he had a viable plan.

4. This car has style, elegance, and is European designed.

5. Dina would either vote for the NDP or the Green Party.

6. Not only did Mark choreograph the ballet, but also wrote the program notes.

7. It is more enjoyable to harvest the vegetables than it is planting them.

8. The flautist walked on stage, performed the concerto, the encore, and walked off the stage to a standing ovation.

9. The horse galloped quickly, smoothly, and without effort.

10. Heathcliff was instructed either to sell his microscopes or ask for more funding.

Correcting faulty parallelism
pp. 227–230

Revise the following sentences in order to repair faulty parallelism.

1. Disagreements over the war were not only apparent between elected officials and voters, but between various elements of the armed forces as well.

2. People adopt roles in life that they are most comfortable with, or will benefit them the most.

3. Not only was our trip like an adventure, but also very much like a marathon.

4. It is significant that the prosecutor ignored the jury and to try to address his comments to the judge.

5. Part of the report is not only concerned with the present situation but also prepares the way for the important reforms that are ahead.

6. We are told that we should eat more fibre, less fat, and exercise regularly.

7. The homeless are a neglected group in our society, and our own lives.

8. About 1750, it became clear to the French that the arrival of the few English traders was only the beginning and soon masses of settlers would follow and overwhelm the French empire in North America.

9. He says that when he graduates he wants to be a teacher, a home owner, and travel.

10. A pet not only gives an older person something to care for, but also a sense of companionship.

11. Today, even newspapers from across the world can be read on the same day of publication via the Internet rather than a magazine shop.

12. The mountaineers had to cope with obsolete or too few pieces of new equipment.

13. The speaker narrates the poem as if he has walked along the streets at night more than once before and that he is acquainted with what goes on around him during his walks.

14. There are many kinds of smiles. For example there are smiles of pleasure, compassion, humour, contempt, winning, competitive, shared secrets, idiotic grins, leers, gloating, sneers, recognition, friendliness, greeting, social, professional, gratification, spontaneous, contagious, deliberate, suppressed, courtesy, anger, humility, rebellion, embarrassment, and surprise.

15. Everything the fortune teller told me was happy and exciting: I would marry an intelligent man, have two children, one who will become a famous author, and the other will be a doctor, travel all over the world, and live until I'm ninety-five, healthy as a young woman.

Using subordination

pp. 230–232

Convert each of the following pairs of sentences into a complex sentence by subordinating one of the original sentences.

1. The book was well written. I did not find it rewarding.

2. The wind was very cold. She wore a heavy sweater.

3. It stopped snowing. We shovelled the driveway.

4. She read a good book. He played solitaire.

5. The meeting was contentious. A consensus was reached.

Correcting faulty coordination
pp. 230–232

Revise the following sentences to eliminate faulty or loose coordination; aim for good subordination, unity, emphasis, and logic. You may also find that you can reduce wordiness.

1. There are no windows in the room, and all lighting is from fluorescent fixtures.

2. At this point Ophelia becomes confused, and this becomes evident when she speaks her next line.

3. Patrick Lewis is a compelling character, and *In the Skin of a Lion* is a great novel about early twentieth-century Toronto.

4. The last appearance of the ghost is in the "closet" scene and the purpose of its appearance is to prevent Hamlet from diverging from his "blunted purpose."

5. Her experiments with chimpanzees were unusual but they were interesting.

6. Older people have already been through what others are experiencing, and this enables them to help.

7. Experts are not always right, and they are seldom wrong.

8. The city's streets are well paved and some of them badly need repair.

9. He is a genius; some people claim that he is an imposter.

10. The stores are usually the first to remind us that Christmas is coming and set the mood with decorations, music, and advertising.

Improving logic
pp. 233–235

Revise the following sentences to eliminate errors in logic.

1. As he approached the shore, he felt a challenge between himself and the sea.

2. Milton's influence on other subsequent poets was very great.

3. Some auto accidents are unavoidable, but can be prevented by proper maintenance.

4. Shakespeare fashioned *A Midsummer Night's Dream* around the theme of love and created the characters and situations to illustrate it in the best possible way. Thus he freely used a variety of comic devices in developing the theme.

5. By the use of imagery, diction, symbolism, and sound, we may also see the structure of the plot.

6. It employed the technique of using projected images on a screen and a corresponding taped conversation which visually enforced the lesson.

7. Throughout history philosophers have been discussing and proposing theories about our purpose on earth, and thus far they can be divided into three general camps.

8. Through the use of too much abstract language, jargon, and clichés, the clarity and effectiveness of this article have been destroyed.

9. As I think back to the days when we were in our early teens, we had a lot of fun together.

10. After his wife died, his paintings of excited forms changed to quiet ones.

Sentence errors and weaknesses

pp. 57–235

The following sentences contain various kinds of errors and weaknesses discussed in parts II, III, and IV. Decide what is wrong with each sentence, label it with the appropriate correction symbol, and then revise the sentence in order to eliminate the problem. Some of the sentences have more than one thing wrong with them.

1. Our coach is overbearing, tall, overpaid, and over forty.

2. One receives this impression when the colour of the picture is considered.

3. Many organic diseases present symptoms that are very similar to autism.

4. Great distances now separate he and his father.

5. The writer's skill was very good.

6. It's true that love and romance come when you least expect it.

7. No player in our school has ever scored as highly as Schmidt did this year.

8. The poem is separated into two parts. The first being his memories and an account of how he reacted to his father's death.

9. Its shape is rounded somewhat resembling a keyhole.

10. I pulled over to the side of the road in a green truck I had borrowed from my roommate, and because the weather was warm I was dressed only in a bathing suit and a bandana, which I had tied around my head.

11. Borelli supposed that there was a tendency for celestial bodies to attract each other but a fluid pressure prevented this.

12. Shakespeare's *Othello* is a brilliant but tragic story of the betrayal of the Moor of Venice by his most trusted lieutenant, Iago.

13. The whole meaning of Housman's poem is that it is better to die young with honour and glory intact than to have someone take it away from you.

14. He says he would like to have another chance at being premier; but if he couldn't run the government right the first time, how can anyone think he's about to do it right again?

15. Smitty is so eager about Michael's friendship, and this is easy to understand even the first time one reads the story.

16. Those who are actually involved in this holiday frenzy may find themselves feeling like getting in touch with old friends, making peace with people they haven't been getting along with, giving to their loved ones and even to strangers, decorating, and enjoying each other's company.

17. They preferred to go out with friends to movies and parties than to stay home and watch TV with their families.

18. By creating an atmosphere of concern for the main character we are more open to the message of the story.

19. What a university stands for more than anything else is an institution where one furthers his education.

20. He has an old worn coat which is far too big for him, but alterations are something he has neither money for nor feels the need to get done.

21. I feel faint; the reason is because I am hungry.

22. Her success is credited to her slyness and wit which always prevails over her daughter's weakness.

23. Physical activity of any kind is always beneficial for the individual.

24. At present the fees are already very expensive.

Part IV: Answers

Section 27a

Example revision: Whitewater rafting is an outdoor activity that is perfect for people looking for an adventure. Several participants will get into a boat and navigate down rivers with different degrees of rough water. While many people think it is exciting, others think it is too dangerous. Experienced guides make the difference because they will show you how to be safe. However, the best guides are the ones that teach you safety while also making sure your experience is exciting.

Section 27b

Example revision: The views of environmentalists and the tourism industry frequently clash over the use of natural areas. Environmentalists know the negative effects an increased human presence can have on remote areas. As a result, they strive to preserve the ecological integrity of these areas. Conversely, the tourism industry points to the often limited economic opportunities in remote areas. They argue that successful tourism can be an excellent revenue source for the remote communities. Finding compromise will not be easy. However, it is possible.

Section 28

Example revision: Ideally, our project will introduce several different learning styles. Although you are almost certainly familiar with one or two of these styles, our project describes the rest. Because the most familiar styles are the easiest to understand, our project begins by outlining them briefly. We continue our project with the less familiar styles. These styles are more abstract. All of them are useful for aspiring teachers, and our project concludes with a list of practical applications.

Sections 27–29

1. Driving up to the campsite, my father chose an empty spot up against the thickly covered mountainside and close to the lake. We were unpacking our equipment and setting up our tent, when an elderly man walked up our path. Introducing himself, he told us that he was camped farther up the mountain, about a hundred yards away, and that walking to his campsite, he saw a huge black bear running away from his campsite. When he got to his campsite, he discovered his tent knocked down and his food scattered all over the ground. With concern for our welfare, he suggested that we may want to move our camp away from this bear's haunts.

2. The sky promised hot and sunny weather. Closing our side-pockets and adjusting our pack straps, we quickly prepared for our hike up Black Tusk in Garibaldi Park. With great enthusiasm for a hike that I had never before travelled, we set off in the early morning light on our first leg of the journey. We would be at the top in a few hours.

3. Our sense of time can change in dramatic circumstances. When I was nine I was hit by a car while I was on my bike. I didn't even see the car, but I heard the screeching brakes. As I flew through the air, I had this odd sensation of floating above the ground, which seemed to come up slowly. Time stopped. Then I hit the ground and time sped up. I was

taken to the hospital and although the whole incident must have taken 20 or 30 minutes, it seemed as though only a minute or two had passed.

4. Repotting a house plant is not so difficult. Assuming it will be too time-consuming and messy, plant-owners procrastinate about repotting. Actually, it takes very little time and effort if you follow a simple set of instructions. Once repotted, your plant, receiving fresh minerals and oxygen from the soil, will grow into a healthier plant. And you will love looking at your thriving plants.

Section 32 (1)

1. (Even when we account for fluctuations in the experiment's key variables.) Even when we account for fluctuations in the experiment's key variables, we obtain similar results.

2. No fragment.

3. (A municipal council subcommittee responsible for road sign replacement.) The young politician earnestly applied herself to her first assignment, a municipal council subcommittee responsible for road sign replacement.

4. (Usable almost anywhere, quiet, non-polluting, and mechanically reliable compared with many other renewable sources.) Solar panels offer several advantages. They are usable almost anywhere, quiet, non-polluting, and mechanically reliable compared with many other renewable sources.

5. (Hungry, dirty, and crying.) We finally found the young boy. He was hungry, dirty, and crying.

6. (Clarissa having purchased the flowers herself.) Clarissa having purchased the flowers herself, the maid continued sleeping.

7. (Asking all who passed by if they needed tickets for the game.) The man stood in front of the stadium asking all who passed by if they needed tickets for the game.

8. (To present the residents with a greater range of services.) To present the residents with a greater range of services, the town council commissioned an addition to the community centre.

9. (Bathurst, Campbellton, Edmunston, Fredericton, and Miramichi.) Bathurst, Campbellton, Edmunston, Fredericton, and Miramichi all have courthouses.

10. (For many cultural anthropologists.) For many cultural anthropologists, ethnographic fieldwork is the quintessential anthropological experience.

Section 32 (2)

(3) **Possible revision**: We discovered it was a spruce grouse, a medium-sized grouse with a long black tail with brown at the end. [Sentences (2) and (3) combined.]

(5) **Possible revision**: There was little food nearby and no undergrowth suitable for nesting.

(8) **Possible revision**: We kept an eye on it through the entire winter, and watched it scratch out an existence. [Sentences (7) and (8) combined.]

(13) **Possible revision**: Because we live in a rural area, we usually let nature take its course. [Sentences (12) and (13) combined.]

(15) **Possible revision**: Our bird appeared too cold and hungry to not leave it something.

(17) **Possible revision**: This is why we decided never to feed the birds in the field again.

Section 35 (1)

1. (badly) The department badly needed funds to teach the students.
2. (that inspired a standing ovation) The duettists that inspired a standing ovation left the stage.
3. (only) If you want to help, be sure to donate to the victims of the floods only through registered charities.
4. (on his phone) Eugene called me from the beach on his phone and asked me if I wanted to go surfing.
5. (covered in her article) Elaina posted links to all of the key topics covered in her article.
6. (that weren't so spicy) Ravi was preparing some dishes that weren't so spicy for his friends.
7. (simply) Already having read the magazines in the waiting room, Sui-Jei simply stared at the ceiling.
8. (that stole the treasure) The thief that stole the treasure was found in the park.
9. (with new green shoes) The skateboarder with new green shoes was excited to get to the skatepark.
10. (nearly) My lemonade stand was so successful this weekend that I made nearly $150.

Section 35 (2)

1. (for two days) For two days, they discussed booking a trip around the world but decided against it.
2. (when I became a parent) I pledged when I became a parent always to listen to my children.
3. (in the morning) In the morning, she decided on this day she would skip dinner entirely.
4. (through the window) Through the window, I could see my grandmother coming.
5. (only) Our submissions were accepted only if they were postmarked by midnight.
6. (only) A piano stood in the centre of the stage with only its outline visible to the audience in the darkness.
7. (only) The newspaper published only three letters to the editor yesterday.
8. (merely) It seemed merely a few days before he returned from his journey to Nepal.

Section 36 (1)

1. (Before turning on the electricity) Before turning on the electricity, she had her wiring diagram inspected.
2. (By performing with a Quebecois group) When he performed with a Quebecois group, his popularity surged.
3. (While resting at the café with our drinks) While we rested at the café with our drinks, a flock of starlings settled on the oak tree.
4. (To fully appreciate Carson's poetry) A familiarity with classical literature allows you to fully appreciate Carson's poetry.
5. (When six years old) When I was six years old, my grandmother opened my eyes to the joys of crochet.
6. (As a leading paleontologist) As a leading paleontologist, the professor counts skeletal reconstruction as an area of expertise.
7. Correct.

8. (Texting often) Texting often, my boyfriend and I have a continuous conversation.
9. Correct.
10. (After finishing the planning) After you finish the planning, the writing is easy.

Section 36 (2)

1. Sitting quiet and fascinated, the baby in her playpen gazed at the hyperactive hummingbird.
2. By using first-person narration, the author leads the readers to wonder about the reliability of the story.
3. Being adept at substituting one ingredient for another, one must be creative in order to cook.
4. Looked at in this light, Hamlet is very much like other people.
5. Réaumur introduced the idea of testing small sample rods and then studying their structure when they are fractured.
6. Being the youngest member of the community, I find it hard to convince the elders of my experience.
7. My activities, when I am not going to school or working, range from playing tennis to surfing the Internet.
8. By using this style, the author added more tension to the dialogue.
9. The colonel began to send groups of reinforcements to the weakened position, reinforcements who were only to be ambushed in the mountain passes.
10. Whispering in the darkened theatre, we spilled our popcorn onto the floor.

Sections 32–36

(1) [mm, *mostly*] . . . lobsters live mostly in a few areas off the east coast.
(2) [dm] Preferring to live in waters with an abundance of rocks and seaweed, most of the lobsters caught in Canada come from the ocean waters . . . .
(3) [mm] In fact, a Nova Scotia fisherman boasts catching the largest lobster on record, which weighed in at just over 20 kilograms.
(4) [cs] . . . valuable seafood export, and it ships these crustaceans . . . .
(5) [run-on] . . . at nearly one billion dollars. They are the primary source of income in many maritime communities.
(6) Ok
(7) [mm, *both*], [cs] In fact, some argue that it is already being overused; however, all levels of government and the people who fish lobster are making efforts to use the resource responsibly.
(8) Ok
(9) [fragment] Female lobsters carrying eggs are also returned to the water.
(10) Ok
(11) [run-on] . . . smaller lobsters are allowed to escape, and they must be made of biodegradable materials so that lobsters aren't trapped if the trap gets lost.
(12) [mm, *only*] We will be able to measure the success of these measures only in future years.

Section 37 (1)

1. The decrease in tourism was due to the fear of terrorism.
2. Soccer happens to be a sport that is very popular in Brazil.
3. I found the children's literature website to be very useful.
4. The new styles were popular with both men and women.
5. Since, for most of us, our earliest recollections are mere fragments of things that made up our childhoods, we must rely on the objects or ideas around us to trigger the past.
6. The popularity of reality television programs is not a sign of a decadent society.

Section 37 (2)

1. A low white blood cell count can mean something is seriously wrong with a patient.
2. Although she is involved in the communist party, she doesn't necessarily hate democracy.
3. Rover is a rambunctious spaniel whose charm increases as he grows older.
4. Increased momentum will alter the trajectory.
5. You are truly wise when you admit you know nothing.
6. The mayor drafted the town council's controversial new plan: an electric barrier.
7. The artists are joining the protest because of the cuts to the papier mâché budget.
8. Observing the results of the study has given us insight into consumer behaviour.

Section 38 (1)

1. The congratulatory speeches at convocation went on for far too long. We listened to them for nearly two hours.
2. The complicated planning process we used to assemble the device was an example of teamwork.
3. Even new psychological theories cannot explain all learning disabilities.
4. Patients can be on a kidney transplant waiting list for months, even years.
5. She failed to satisfy the teacher with her restraint.
6. Some people use alcohol to escape from reality.
7. Many of the forty-six guilty verdicts in the month of July resulted from what the legal system calls "driving under the influence."
8. Fortunately, the news that Meredith was anxiously expecting arrived.
9. Feed the paper into this photocopier one sheet at a time.
10. The office temperature, once adjusted by hand, is now controlled electronically.

Section 38 (2)

1. I decided not to buy it, for it was too expensive.
2. Despite the upheaval, people were undergoing spiritual enlightenment during this period.
3. Clearly, his ability is greatly underestimated.
4. The only light in the house came through the windows.
5. It is a rectangle.
6. The poem expresses the meaninglessness of war.
7. The speaker in the poem is euphoric and energetic.

8. The effort required in reading the text indicates a weakness in the writing.

9. The idea of life and death was constantly in the pioneers' minds.

10. She was very young when she started university.

Section 39

1. Leslie had been training for months before the rugby coach invited her to try out for the team.

2. Her letter said that years ago the farmers had wanted to build a facility for converting manure into saleable methane, but financial woes made that impossible.

3. I took the bus to the museum and saw Belinda walking out with Stuart.

4. If you want to learn how to play piano, you must be dedicated because you have to practice every day.

5. When the firefighters arrived at the burning building, the roof had erupted into flames.

6. Read the first chapter of the book and answer each of the questions provided.

7. If you don't follow a healthy diet, you can suffer a stroke or heart attack.

8. Although some people see the values in these regulations, others do not.

9. When you write back, please let me know if you have any questions.

10. We tool and die makers take pride in our trade, and we always complete our projects on schedule.

Section 40 (1)

1. When plotting other ships on the map, you should consider their speed, direction, and location.

2. Our new application is designed for retrieving data, creating files, and compressing information.

3. Gustaff showed his professor he had sufficient funding and a viable plan.

4. This car has style, elegance, and European design.

5. Dina would vote for either the NDP or the Green Party.

6. Not only did Mark choreograph the ballet, but he also wrote the program notes.

7. It is more enjoyable to harvest the vegetables than it is to plant them.

8. The flautist stepped on stage, performed the concerto as well as an encore, and walked off the stage to a standing ovation.

9. The horse galloped quickly, smoothly, and effortlessly.

10. Heathcliff was instructed to either sell his microscopes or ask for more funding.

Section 40 (2)

1. Disagreements over the war were not only apparent between elected officials and voters, but were also apparent between various elements of the armed forces as well.

2. People adopt roles in life that they are most comfortable with or that they will benefit from the most.

3. Not only was our trip like an adventure, but it was also very much like a marathon.

4. It is significant that the prosecutor ignored the jury and tried to address his comments to the judge.

5. Part of the report is not only concerned with the present situation but it also prepares the

way for the important reforms that are ahead.

6. We are told that we should eat more fibre, eat less fat, and exercise regularly.

7. The homeless are a neglected group in our society and in our own lives.

8. About 1750, it became clear to the French that the arrival of the few English traders was only the beginning and that soon masses of settlers would follow and overwhelm the French empire in North America.

9. He says that when he graduates he wants to be a teacher, a home owner, and a traveller.

10. A pet not only gives an older person something to care for, but also gives this person a sense of companionship.

11. Today, newspapers from across the world can be read on the same day of publication via the Internet rather than read several days later in the magazine shop.

12. The mountaineers had to cope with obsolete or old equipment.

13. The speaker narrates the poem as if he has walked along the streets at night more than once before and as if he is acquainted with what goes on around him during his walks.

14. There are many kinds of smiles. For example, there are smiles that indicate pleasure, compassion, humour, contempt, shared secrets, gloating, recognition, friendliness, gratification, spontaneity, suppressed courtesy, anger, humility, rebellion, embarrassment, and surprise.

15. Everything the fortune teller told me was happy and exciting: I would marry an intelligent man; I would have two children, one who will become a famous author and the other will become a doctor; I would travel all over the world; and I would live until I'm ninety-five as healthy as a young woman.

Section 41 (1)

1. Although the book was well written, I did not find it rewarding.

2. She wore a heavy sweater because the wind was very cold.

3. When it stopped snowing, we shovelled the driveway.

4. While she read a good book, he played solitaire.

5. Even though the meeting was contentious, a consensus was reached.

Section 41 (2)

1. Because there are no windows in the room, all lighting is from fluorescent fixtures.

2. At this point, Ophelia's confusion becomes evident when she speaks her next line.

3. *In the Skin of a Lion*, a great novel about early twentieth-century Toronto, features a compelling character, Patrick Lewis.

4. The last appearance of the ghost, occurring in the "closet" scene, prevents Hamlet from diverging from his "blunted purpose."

5. Her experiments with chimpanzees were unusual and interesting.

6. Older people, having already been through what others are experiencing, are able to help.

7. Experts may not always be right, but they are seldom wrong.

8. Although some of them badly need repair, the city's streets for the most part are well paved.

9. He is a genius; however, some people claim that he is an imposter.

10. The stores are usually the first to remind us that Christmas is coming by setting the mood with decorations, music, and advertising.

Section 42

1. As he approached the shore, he felt that the sea was challenging him.
2. Subsequent poets were greatly influenced by Milton.
3. Some auto accidents can be avoided by proper car maintenance.
4. Love is the theme of Shakespeare's *A Midsummer Night's Dream*. The characters, situations, and variety of comic devices develop this theme in the best possible way.
5. The structure of the plot can be seen in the imagery, diction, symbolism, and sound.
6. Visually enforcing the lesson, it projected images on a screen and played a corresponding taped conversation.
7. Throughout history, philosophers, who can be divided into three general camps, have been discussing and proposing theories about our purpose on earth.
8. Too much abstract language, jargon, and clichés have destroyed the clarity and effectiveness of this article.
9. I remember we had a lot of fun together when we were teenagers.
10. After his wife died, his paintings changed from energetic forms to subdued ones.

Review exercises: Parts II, III, and IV

1. Our coach is overbearing, overpaid, and over forty. (faulty logic and parallelism)
2. The colour of the picture makes this impression. (passive voice and wordiness)
3. Many organic diseases have symptoms similar to those of autism. (faulty logic)
4. Great distances now separate him and his father. (incorrect pronoun usage)
5. The writer was skillful. (logic—It is the skill that makes the writer good.)
6. Love and romance come when you least expect them. (wordy)
7. No player in our school has scored as many points as Schmidt did this year. (incorrect modifier)
8. The poem is separated into two parts: his memories and his reaction to his father's death. (emphasis needed)
9. It has a keyhole shape. (wordy)
10. I pulled over to the side of the road in my roommate's green truck; because of the heat, I was wearing only a bathing suit and a head bandana. (emphasis and variety needy)
11. Borelli supposed that the tendency for celestial bodies to attract each other was prevented by fluid pressure. (weak expletive)
12. Shakespeare's *Othello* is a brilliant and tragic story of the betrayal of the Moor of Venice, Othello, by his most trusted lieutenant, Iago. (logic and alignment)
13. Housman's poem tells us that it is better to die young with honour and glory intact than to have these qualities taken away. (wordy)
14. He says he would like to have another chance of being premier; but if he couldn't run the government effectively the first time, how can anyone think he can run it effectively this time? (word choice and logic can be questioned—faulty generalization)
15. On first reading, the reader understands that Smitty is eager for Michael's friendship. (emphasis needed through clause combination)
16. Those involved in this holiday frenzy may find themselves enjoying the company of others by getting in touch with old friends, making peace with people, and giving to loved ones and strangers. (logical grouping)

17. They preferred to go out with friends to movies and parties rather than stay at home watching television with their families. (faulty parallelism)

18. We are more open to the message of the story because the writer engages our sympathy for the main character. (dangling modifier)

19. A university is an institution where people further their education. (inclusive language)

20. He does not have the money or inclination to alter his big old worn coat. (faulty parallelism)

21. I feel faint because I am hungry. (mixed construction)

22. She is successful because her slyness and wit prevails over her daughter's weakness. (wordy)

23. Any physical activity benefits the individual. (wordy)

24. Currently, the fees are too high. (wordy—overuse of modifiers)

Part V
Punctuation

The comma, independent clauses, and coordinating conjunctions
pp. 240–242

Insert a comma to correct the following sentences. You may decide that some need no punctuation. Could some be punctuated in more than one way?

Example: Ethanol creates lower GHG emissions than gasoline, but some agriculture experts argue its production requires too much farmland to be sustainable.

1. You can sit in the bleachers or you can stand at the stage.

2. The law and morality are generally viewed as being separate but related realms but this is only superficially accurate.

3. Widows receive pensions from the government but separated and divorced women do not.

4. The photographers combed through a year's worth of work and came up with their favourite photos.

5. The families moved in the artists left.

6. There should be little surprise at the relocation of several factories for manufacturers need access to reliable electric power.

7. Many patients experienced painful side effects so doctors began designing alternative treatments.

8. Bat populations decreased and mosquito populations increased.

9. Oil and gas exploration is risky business anywhere yet Newfoundland is experiencing a mini-boom.

10. Deviance is upsetting and perplexing and it confronts people in many settings.

Punctuating parallel adjectives and series
pp. 242–243

Punctuate the following sentences as necessary.

1. The things I expected from my education were maturity spiritual growth and a career.

2. The zookeeper gave a mixture of pork venison and rice to the excited male hyenas.

3. Parsnips sardines and peanut butter were the ingredients for my new culinary creation.

4. Running campaigns communicating with constituents and drafting legislation are just three parts of a politician's job.

5. The cheerful conscientious young man wore an elegant black suit to the gala.

6. Quickly quietly and discreetly Rhya left the auditorium.

7. Nico suggests a better more even-handed approach to disciplining children teens and college students.

8. We installed the expensive research computer in a lab where only trained qualified undergraduates could access it.

Punctuating adverbial clauses
pp. 244–247

Insert commas where you think necessary in the following sentences. Indicate any places where you think a comma would be optional.

1. Although it was almost midnight he knew he had to stay up and finish writing the report.

2. You may begin now if you want to.

3. You may begin whenever you wish.

4. The snowboarding is especially good this year because the snow is plentiful.

5. Because the snow is plentiful this year the snowboarding is especially good.

6. Before you move to Paris you should study French.

7. Sleeping in on the weekend is a fundamental right though my family does not recognize the fact.

8. Some people can tell where commas are required when they read the sentences aloud and listen for the natural pauses.

9. After Anne finished the report which showed marked improvement in profits she seemed less happy than she had before she began the report.

10. However you look at it the solution needs to be simple and practical or the boss will not approve of it.

Punctuating opening and closing words and phrases
pp. 244–247

Insert commas where you think necessary in the following sentences. Indicate any places where you think a comma would be optional.

1. In December my family always goes skiing.

2. We walked slowly soaking up the sights and sounds along the waterfront.

3. At the end of the lecture I had no clearer understanding of the subject than I had when I came in.

4. The dog walked and fed I decided to relax with a murder mystery.

5. The brain regulates and integrates our senses allowing us to experience our environment.

6. Raising prices results in increased wage demands adding to inflation.

7. Following the instructions I poured the second chemical into the beaker with the first and shook them shutting my eyes in the expectation of something unpleasant.

8. As usual before going to bed I turned on the eleven o'clock news.

9. To make a long story short I found my aunt looking healthier than I'd ever seen her before.

10. Looking pop-eyed and furious the coach stared back at the referee without saying a word.

Punctuating words, phrases, and adverbial clauses
pp. 244–247

Punctuate the following sentences. Indicate where a comma would be optional, and indicate any sentences that would be correct without adding any punctuation with a check mark.

1. The oil company having just built it refused to close down the refinery.

2. Since becoming a lawyer Logan has had little time for his stamp collection.

3. Adhering to a special diet is common for athletes preparing for a competition.

4. For this weekend Fisher & Co. is planning a retreat.

5. The instructor was ill the day of the test thankfully.

6. After we introduced the new format the old one became obsolete.

7. The opposition centred its election campaign on a platform of tax reductions and rebates, taxes having increased under the current government.

8. In order to represent all of the different types of responses to the question visually I have prepared this graph.

9. Feeling dejected Donald grumbled the whole trip to the circus.

10. A corresponding increase in unit cost however affects purchasing behaviour.

Punctuating nonrestrictive elements
pp. 247–251

Decide whether the italicized elements in the following sentences are restrictive or nonrestrictive, and insert punctuation as required.

1. The student *who takes studying seriously* is the one *who is most likely to succeed.*

2. The novels *I like best* are those page turners *you can buy at the drugstore.*

3. This movie *which was produced on a very low budget* was a popular success.

4. Whitehorse *the capital of Yukon* has a thriving arts community.

5. Pliny *the Elder* wrote about some interesting herbal remedies *involving bat dung and garlic.*

6. Sentence interrupters *such as parenthetical definitions* should be set off with commas.

7. Michel Tremblay *the playwright* is a Quebec writer with a national reputation.

8. Life of Pi *written by Yann Martel* is about a boy and a tiger on a lifeboat.

9. My twin brother *Greg* is very proud of his partner *Martin.*

10. In the view of the small-town newspaper editor *James Borred* the 12-foot worm was nothing to get excited about.

Identifying and punctuating nonrestrictive and restrictive elements
pp. 247–251

Insert commas into the following sentences. Explain the cases in which the commas are optional.

1. Give the secret documents only to the woman who is wearing the fuchsia sweater.

2. My friend Paul who was sending me postcards all summer is the only person I know who has been to Nigeria.

3. The French army with hopes of fortifying its last remaining stronghold retreated behind the city walls.

4. Bonsai trees which require great attention and patience are not naturally so small.

5. The president of the company David is the only person who can make that decision.

6. The left winger a recent addition to the team has already scored a team-leading twelve goals this season.

7. Leena who has an interest in computers wants to get a diploma in graphic design.

8. One of McLuhan's most quoted books *Understanding Media* was published in 1964.

9. The tree you want to focus most of your attention on is the maple.

10. Vancouver's First Narrows Bridge better known as the Lions Gate Bridge connects the downtown area to the north shore.

Using commas

pp. 239–251

Insert commas to correct the following sentences. You may decide that some need no punctuation. Could some be punctuated in more than one way?

1. Others such as political activists may be arrested several times for their activities yet they continue to protest.

2. The stories they tell the characters they portray and the stereotypes they convey shape and reflect our popular culture.

3. His wife Candice believed children should be introduced to different types of music.

4. Despite the controversies and despite the passions they usually unleash rights and freedoms have had a low profile in Canadian politics for most of this country's history.

5. The second graph on the other hand indicates some of the consequences of providing informal care to an older person.

6. A great challenge for students is then to create a picture book for their siblings or for younger grades in the school.

7. Amal is captain of the hockey team and he is also a graceful athletic figure skater.

8. Mobile communications have made it possible for employees to be part of virtual project teams which can eliminate time and space barriers and still provide quality low-cost solutions to organizational problems.

Extra punctuation practice: the comma
pp. 239–251

Add necessary commas to the following sentences. If the sentence does not require any punctuation, place a check mark beside it.

1. Katie who seems to excel at any sport she tries has also signed up for the water-polo team.

2. My roommate wrote a poem and it was published in the college's only literary journal *Stanza.*

3. The evidence in the second article however is much more damning.

4. Elm Maple and Beech trees lined the main street in Woodstock Ontario.

5. Gaston is taking introductory French but his teacher Madame Denis suspects he should be in the other class that she teaches which meets on Monday.

6. A new department at the university Nanotechnology will attract more students inspire new research and enlarge the engineering faculty.

7. Rasheed will you at least help us put up one of the tents or a tarpaulin?

8. Failing to anticipate the volume of sales the company quickly ran out of inventory.

9. I missed on my first attempt but I tried again after being encouraged by Thomas one of the other competitors.

10. The women distributed pamphlets to all who passed by even those who initially refused and half the town had read their manifesto by the end of the day.

11. So many home owners occupy the council that renters are barely represented.

12. My friend Kayleigh is travelling to Moose Jaw Saskatchewan because her father lives there and she has not seen him in a very long time.

The semicolon

pp. 252–255

Add semicolons where appropriate and/or other necessary punctuation to the blanks in the following sentences. Could some be punctuated in more than one way?

Example: Radiocarbon dating of evidence suggests that Easter Island was settled by the seventh century ; the first settlers were likely Polynesians , not South Americans.

1. I am not sure_ but I think I'm in the wrong tutorial_ I will find out tomorrow.

2. Some people may see an area of wetland as a valuable scientific or recreational landscape_ others will see it as potential farm or building land.

3. Besides the immediate recipients of your expense report_ there may be several other readers, including your supervisor_ the financial controller of the company_ or a budget committee.

4. One group claims that travel and tourism account for about $5.9 trillion of economic activity_ which is about 10 per cent of global GDP.

5. Dictionaries also have entries for phrases, including idioms_ look under the main word in the expression.

6. Firefighters had the trust of 97 per cent of Canadians in 2012_ nurses, 94 per cent_ teachers, 89 per cent_ and police officers, 84 per cent.

7. The imaginative work of the reader_ however_ remains the same for historical fiction as for fantasy.

8. The opening paragraph introduces not only the essay but also its writer_ therefore_ you must appear credible and reliable.

9. Even the dead of this city cannot rest in peace_ their bones are dug up by desperate children and sold to bone-dealers.

Comma, semicolon, or colon
pp. 239–256

Insert whatever punctuation mark (other than a period) you think works best between the independent clauses in the following sentences. You may decide that some need no punctuation. Could some be punctuated in more than one way?

1. Everyone thought the technological revolution would reduce our use of paper we were wrong.

2. Jamil needed some help with his lab report so he thought he would make an appointment with a tutor.

3. Cartoons are enjoyed by both children and adults sometimes adults enjoy them more.

4. Some people eat to live others live to eat.

5. It was a fascinating hypothesis but it was greeted with silence.

6. His belly shook he had a red nose he was surrounded by reindeer.

7. The hurricane warning went up and most people sauntered to their shelters others continued to watch TV.

8. Easy come easy go.

9. You live you learn.

10. The strike was over the people were jubilant.

Using the semicolon, colon, and dash
pp. 252–258

Determine if the semicolon, colon, and dash used in the following sentences is appropriate or inappropriate. For questions where punctuation has been used inappropriately, provide a correction.

1. The particular policy positions adopted—or, alternatively, rejected—could have the potential to influence the global balance of prosperity.

2. Kate chooses an apple; Iain chooses a deep-fried chocolate bar.

3. We left the market—after driving for fifteen minutes, we arrived home with— our groceries.

4. Who should own the Rosetta Stone: Should it be the English?

5. The next time they do—something like this—bring out the fire trucks and hose them all down.

6. Individuals are expected to fall back on the earnings of other family members; families with children are given special consideration.

7. Mario got a speeding ticket, told a lie; and dug himself in deeper.

8. Marx identified culture as an extension of capitalism's economic base; in other words, he thought culture simply stated the values of capitalism as doctrine.

9. Nada revealed the revolutionary component of her new design: a four-way catalytic converter.

10. Please call our booking agency—Funambulists Incorporated about hiring us for your next event.

Punctuating sentence interrupters
pp. 251, 256–259

Set off the italicized interrupters with commas, dashes, or parentheses. Be prepared to defend your choices.

1. It was seven o'clock in the evening *a mild autumn evening* and the crickets were beginning to chirp.

2. No one *at least no one who was present* wanted to disagree with the speaker's position.

3. Early one Sunday morning *a morning I will never forget* the phone rang unexpectedly.

4. Since it was only a mild interjection *no more than a barely audible snort from the back of the room* he went on with scarcely a pause but with a slightly raised eyebrow and finished his speech.

5. And then suddenly *out of the blue and into my head* came the only possible answer.

Correcting comma splices and run-on sentences
pp. 270–271 (p. 215)

Correct any comma splices and run-on sentences in the following examples.

1. I had not been back in ages therefore I was surprised to see all the changes.

2. We started to edit the next edition of the newsletter, soon the office was littered with coffee cups and paper.

3. Atwood uses figurative language, however the literal sense is sufficiently clear.

4. But we sat silent the scene before us on the stage had left us stunned.

5. They make faces at each other each time they pass on the street.

6. This sales letter doesn't acknowledge women exist therefore they will never buy the product.

7. Life in those days was a gruelling chore, but at least life was short.

8. The dictator's statue stood for almost thirty years however it was toppled in less than an hour.

9. We pushed off from the shore the canoes were buffeted by the waves we found ourselves unexpectedly in the water.

10. Things went suspiciously well the first person to look at the house wanted to buy it.

Correcting comma splices and run-on sentences
pp. 270–271 (p. 215)

Identify each of the following examples as either a comma splice error or a run-on sentence. Suggest a revision. If the sentence is already correct, place a check mark beside it.

Example: Coming up with ideas is easy writing is difficult. *Run-on*

        Coming up with ideas is easy, but writing is difficult.

1. Ann-Marie MacDonald is well known as a novelist and she also writes plays.

   _____

2. Alison needed visuals for her poster, however, only maps of other areas were available. _____

3. His diagnosis was serious, but he was expected to make an eventual recovery.

   _____

4. The mechanics, although they started late, have promised to finish the job, they will get your car back on the road. _____

5. We knew the solution, already very potent, would get even stronger if we added the crystals so we poured them in. _____

6. The inconsiderate women spilled crumbs all over the table and chairs while they ate their muffins and drank their overpriced cappuccinos. _____

7. Known for her fairness, the bank manager promised her staff raises or she would improve their benefits. _____

8. They looked angry when they arrived we packed up and left, disappointed to give up the field. _____

9. The trumpet player took a solo, the band behind him was sounding amazing. _____

10. Because frogs breathe partially through their skin they are sensitive to pollution and they indicate of environmental health. _____

Correcting comma splices and run-on sentences
pp. 270–271 (p. 215)

Identify the comma splice errors and run-on sentences in the following paragraphs. Suggest a revision for the errors.

(1) Many Canadians have heard Roberta Bondar's name, some of us might know she was an astronaut, but we do not know anything else about her.

(2) Roberta Bondar went to space in 1992 aboard space shuttle *Discovery*. (3) She was Canada's first female astronaut, additionally, she was the first neurologist in space. (4) While on the mission she carried out many experiments, and she has since become globally recognized for her achievements in space medicine. (5) She has not been in space the whole time but her research for over a decade has examined the way astronauts recover from microgravity of space. (6) She has discovered important connections between the way astronauts recover and neurological illnesses such as Parkinson's disease.

(7) Bondar's achievements in space are many, she has also been very busy on Earth. (8) She is a passionate environmentalist, and she has worked hard to inform and advise individuals, companies, and governments and improving environmental education in secondary and elementary schools has been one of her biggest efforts.

(9) She is also an author, public speaker, acclaimed photographer, and until 2009, she was the chancellor of Trent University in Ontario, what an incredible woman!

With information from *Roberta Bondar: Navigating Uncharted Territory*. Roberta Bondar Astronaut Enterprise, 2009. Web. 11 Jan. 2013. <www.robertabondar.com>.

Extra punctuation practice

pp. 239–258

Insert commas, semicolons, dashes, and colons where you think necessary in the following sentences. If no changes are required, place a check mark beside the sentence.

1. The first stanza describes a series of seemingly unconnected items a pair of sandals a ship's hull a wooden dresser and twenty-five truffles.

2. L.M. Montgomery's novel *The Story Girl* is my favourite book however *Anne of Green Gables* also has a special place in my heart.

3. Social rituals such as funerals and marriages are important they create cohesion.

4. Rahiq having discovered the source of the problem immediately started thinking of solutions.

5. She walked through the hallway pausing to admire the artwork on the walls.

6. When Susan returned it to her the pashmina scarf the precious gift that her sister had brought back for her all the way from Kathmandu was ripped.

7. Zacharias Kunuk worked for the Inuit Broadcasting Corporation started his own production company and released several documentaries and short dramas but his most recognized achievement was his full-length movie *Atanarjuat*.

8. His mother who went to university in Pakistan before coming to Canada is a professor of pure mathematics at the university.

9. Knowing what he did of the owner's character he could only see one motive driving the recent round of layoffs greed.

10. Being able to say he had visited the capitals of all ten provinces and three territories was a source of great pride for Mohsen.

Quotation marks

pp. 264–268

Add quotation marks to the following sentences. Indicate where these marks are optional.

1. When asked about her favourite sports, the young woman said, I only enjoy watching basketball, soccer, and tennis.

2. The instructor warned her students, I don't want to hear a single electronic beep.

3. What about my Blackberry? asked Larry. Does it count?

4. Hamlet's most recognized soliloquy begins to be or not to be.

5. Roberta said, Juliet claims that she wasn't there.

6. Macdonald's discontent is evident in his journals: The progress of this government is slow and nearly intolerable.

7. Two notable examples of hockey in Canadian literature are Michael Ondaatje's poem To a Sad Daughter and Wayne Johnston's short story collection *Original Six*.

8. We later found out that our professor's field research excursions were actually week-long drinking benders.

9. The new hospitals will be built after 2011, replied the government's spokesperson.

10. Has no one here read Dorothy Livesay's poem The Three Emilys? asked the poetry society president exasperatedly.

11. Joseph assumed there would be evidence that the results had been faked.

Punctuation review

pp. 239–277

Insert any necessary punctuation into the following paragraphs.

Lake Winnipeg is the tenth-largest freshwater lake in the world Even more impressive its watershed is the second largest in Canada and includes large areas of four provinces Ontario Manitoba Alberta and Saskatchewan and two states North Dakota and Minnesota A rapid rate of replenishment and a shallow depth the average for the entire lake is only 12 metres make the lake especially habitable for fish The lake helps to make Manitoba the second-largest freshwater fishery in Canada and its abundance of walleye a popular sport fish brings thousands of anglers to the lake every year In fact Lake Winnipeg is one of Manitoba's primary recreational resources attracting not just anglers but tourists who come for the natural beauty of the lake and the excellent boating hiking cycling and camping that it offers

In recent years concern about the ecological health of the lake has increased Surprisingly the biggest threat is a naturally occurring plant blue-green algae The overgrowth of this plant which is extremely harmful to ecosystems is the result of human practices within the watershed Agricultural runoff and sewage from cities and towns flow into the lake eventually overloading the lake water with phosphorus and nitrogen These two elements act as fertilizer and create unnaturally large algae blooms which deplete the oxygen that the lake's ecosystem needs to function naturally The blooms can devastate a fish population Additionally they are toxic and can force the closure of beaches to people Because of the importance of the fishery and tourism to the Manitoba economy the government is starting to work to protect the lake however it must act quickly and before it is too late

With information from the following sources:

Great Canadian Lakes. Canoe Inc., 2012. Web. 11 Jan. 2013. <www.greatcanadianlakes.com>.

A Sea of Troubles: Lake Winnipeg in Crisis. CBC/Radio Canada, 2009. Web. 21 Apr. 2009. <www.cbc.ca/manitoba/features/lakewinnipeg/>.

Punctuation review
pp. 239–277

In the following paragraphs, correct any misused punctuation and insert any necessary punctuation that is missing.

Some people ask, who were Canada's Famous Five? They were five women from Alberta who changed the political life of women in Canada: Emily Murphy, a social activist, Nellie McClung, a novelist and journalist, Louise McKinney, a politician, Irene Parlby, also a politician, and Henrietta Muir Edwards, a journalist. They were all involved in women's suffrage, but their most widely recognized achievement, came in the late 1920s—through what is know as the "Persons" Case. The efforts of these five women, in the case which took place between 1927 and 1929, resulted in women gaining the legal ability to sit in the Senate.

The reason it became known as the "Persons" Case was its focus on use of the word in section twenty-four of *The British North America Act* which refers to the "persons" eligible to sit in the Senate. The Famous Five took the bold step of asking the Supreme Court of Canada, to clarify the document. It may seem odd—at least to most "persons" today that this was even something that required clarification. However in its initial 1927 ruling, the Court rejected the idea that "persons" included women. It said, that *The BNA Act* was drafted in 1867 when women did not hold political office, therefore, when its authors wrote "persons," they meant "men" The Famous Five were not satisfied with this response, and appealed the decision to the highest court of appeal possible, the Judicial Committee of England's Privy Council. Their appeal was successful, the Judicial Committee ruling unanimously that women were allowed to hold seats in the senate.

Although none of the Famous Five ever became senators, the first female senator Cairine Wilson was admitted to the Canadian Senate, only four months after the Five's successful appeal. In 2013, there were over thirty female members of the senate, the work of the Famous Five was an important early step in the struggle for equality, and their efforts continue to inspire people who seek equal social, economic, and political rights today. Recently, a monument on Parliament Hill in Ottawa Ontario—was erected to commemorate their contribution to the lives of all Canadians.

Punctuation review
pp. 239–277

A. CORRECTING PUNCTUATION

Correct any errors in punctuation in the following sentences—many of which come from students' papers. You may also want to make other improvements: practise your revising techniques.

1. Rainer Maria Rilke says love occurs when two solitudes protect and touch and greet each other.

2. I believe, that for a number of reasons, genetically modified food should be carefully regulated.

3. He was not a frightening poltergeist but an irritating one he hid the remote control and moved the coffee table.

4. Many of his plays are about royalty, as in the Lancastrian tetralogy *Richard II Henry IV* (1) *Henry IV* (2) and *Henry V*.

5. His childlike features were deceptive as we discovered when the alien from the planet Zotar began to give us detailed instructions on how to build a time machine.

6. When you spend time with close friends you get a different perspective life seems less narrow and serious.

7. With him too, she felt comfortable.

8. I would like to wake up in the morning especially a beautiful morning such as this and not feel the burden of work.

9. The encounter that deepened his feelings more, occurred at age nine.

10. Therefore one must always remember to be polite when encountering a ghostly stranger in a train station.

11. This then, was the plan. Return to our campsite for the night, and tackle Black Tusk the next morning.

12. I joined in; dancing haltingly at first and then more confidently.

13. As a person exercises the muscle of the heart becomes stronger therefore, it can pump more blood while beating less.

14. However I always wake up the next day with the worst sort of headache the emotional headache.

15. The meal started with grilled artichokes followed by mushroom ravioli and finished with a lemon tart.

16. It was after all, exactly what he had asked for.

17. Crisp memories of laughing eyes, loving smiles and peaceful easy feelings still linger.

18. A computer hard drive is easy to install just remember to ground yourself before you touch the hard drive.

19. Did Sheila Watson write *The Double Hook*.

20. Eighteenth-century mathematicians unlike their counterparts in the seventeenth century, were able to develop both pure and applied mathematics. Leonhard Euler, a notable genius in both these fields contributed invaluably to every branch of mathematics.

21. Another classic film, that explores the effects of war on individual lives, is *Casablanca*.

22. It began to rain, nevertheless, since they were on the sixteenth fairway they went ahead and finished the round.

23. When the tyrant stood up and said you rascals you will get what you deserve a brick fell on his head.

24. To me this indicates, that although he remembers the details of the events he describes, there is an enormous space of time, between them and the present, that makes them intangible.

25. The sounds of the sonata are soft and never harsh which helps create the melancholy mood.

B. USING PUNCTUATION

Punctuate the following sentences as you think best, indicating possible alternatives and places where you think punctuation is optional. Be prepared to defend your choices. Some sentences may not need punctuating.

1. When the meeting ended he went to a pub for a drink.

2. Doggedly Peyvand finished his essay.

3. Soon those parts became unappealing and she decided to fire her current agent.

4. In 2000 he moved to Halifax Nova Scotia and bought a small reputable art gallery specializing in expensive striking white minimalist plastic sculpture.

5. She felt uneasy about the trip yet she knew she had to go and meet her sister flying in from Hong Kong.

6. I took the book that I didn't like back to the library but I still had to pay a fine.

7. Mary Winnie and Cora came to the party together but left separately.

8. He had a broad engaging smile even though he had three teeth missing.

9. Having heard all she wanted Bridget walked out of the meeting.

10. But once you've taken the first few steps the rest will naturally be easy.

11. The poem was short the novel was long the poem was good the novel better.

12. Perhaps we can still think of some way out of this mess.

13. But Canadians don't think that way they prefer to sit back and wait.

14. Last summer we visited Hastings the site of the battle won by William the Conqueror in 1066.

15. A warm bath a good book and freshly laundered sheets were all she wanted.

16. There are only three vegetables I can't tolerate turnips turnips and turnips.

17. In the good old days the doctor a specialist in family practice made house calls all morning.

18. August 16 1977 is when Elvis Presley died.

19. He had to finish the novel quickly or he wouldn't get his advance.

20. We arrived we ate we partook in boring conversation we departed and that's all there was to the evening.

21. You must plan your budget carefully in times of inflation so remember to buy lottery tickets.

22. She is the only woman I know who wears pantyhose every day whatever the season.

23. His several hobbies were philately woodworking chess and fishing.

24. The two opponents settled the question amicably at the meeting and then went home to write nasty letters to each other and to the editor of the local newspaper.

25. He would rather make up a lie than stick to the boring truth that was his downfall.

Part V: Answers

Section 43a–b

1. You can sit in the bleachers, or you can stand at the stage.
2. The law and morality are generally viewed as being separate but related realms, but this is only superficially accurate.
3. Widows receive pensions from the government, but separated and divorced women do not.
4. Correct.
5. The families moved in, the artists left. **OR** The families moved in. **T**he artists left.
6. There should be little surprise at the relocation of several factories, for manufacturers need access to reliable electric power.
7. Many patients experienced painful side effects, so doctors began designing alternative treatments.
8. Bat populations decreased, and mosquito populations increased. **OR** Correct.
9. Oil and gas exploration is risky business anywhere, yet Newfoundland is experiencing a mini-boom.
10. Deviance is upsetting and perplexing, and it confronts people in many settings,

Section 43c–d

1. The things I expected from my education were maturity, spiritual growth, and a career.
2. The zookeeper gave a mixture of pork, venison, and rice to the excited male hyenas.
3. Parsnips, sardines, and peanut butter were the ingredients for my new culinary creation.
4. Running campaigns, communicating with constituents, and drafting legislation are just three parts of a politician's job.
5. The cheerful, conscientious young man wore an elegant black suit to the gala.
6. Quickly, quietly, and discreetly Rhya left the auditorium.
7. Nico suggests a better, more even-handed approach to disciplining children, teens, and college students.
8. We installed the expensive research computer in a lab where only trained, qualified undergraduates could access it.

Section 43e (1)

1. Although it was almost midnight, he knew he had to stay up and finish writing the report.
2. No change needed
3. No change needed
4. No change needed
5. Because the snow is plentiful this year, the snowboarding is especially good.
6. Before you move to Paris, you should study French.
7. Sleeping in on the weekend is a fundamental right, though my family does not recognize the fact.
8. No change needed
9. After Anne finished the report, which showed marked improvement in profits, she seemed less happy than she had before she began the report.
10. However you look at it, the solution needs to be simple and practical, or the boss will not

approve of it.

Section 43e (2)

1. In December, my family always goes skiing. [comma is optional]
2. We walked slowly, soaking up the sights and sounds along the waterfront.
3. At the end of the lecture, I had no clearer understanding of the subject than I had when we came in.
4. The dog walked and fed, I decided to relax with a murder mystery.
5. The brain regulates and integrates our senses, allowing us to experience our environment.
6. Raising prices results in increased wage demands, adding to inflation.
7. Following the instructions, I poured the second chemical into the beaker with the first and shook them, shutting my eyes in the expectation of something unpleasant.
8. As usual, before going to bed, I turned on the eleven o'clock news. [The first comma after *usual* is optional.]
9. To make a long story short, I found my aunt looking healthier than I'd ever seen her before.
10. Looking pop-eyed and furious, the coach stared back at the referee without saying a word.

Sections 43e (3)

1. The oil company, having just built it, refused to close down the refinery.
2. Since becoming a lawyer, Logan has little time for his stamp collection.
3. Correct.
4. For this weekend, Fisher & Co. is planning a retreat.
5. The instructor was ill the day of the test, thankfully.
6. After we introduced the new format, the old one became obsolete.
7. Correct.
8. In order to represent all of the different types of responses to the question visually, I have prepared this graph.
9. Feeling dejected, Donald grumbled the whole trip to the circus.
10. A corresponding increase in unit cost, however, affects purchasing behaviour.

Section 43f (1)

1. Both clauses are restrictive, so no commas should be added.
2. Both clauses are restrictive, so no commas should be added.
3. This movie, *which was produced on a very low budget*, was a popular success.
   The clause is nonrestrictive, so it should be enclosed in commas.
4. Whitehorse, *the capital of Yukon*, has a thriving arts community.
   The phrase is nonrestrictive, so it should be enclosed in commas.
5. Both phrases are restrictive, so no commas should be added.
6. The phrase is restrictive, so no commas should be added.
7. Michel Tremblay, *the playwright*, is a Quebec writer with a national reputation.

The phrase is nonrestrictive, so it should be enclosed in commas.

8. <u>Life of Pi</u>, *written by Yann Martel*, is about a boy and a tiger on a lifeboat.

    The phrase is nonrestrictive, so it should be enclosed in commas.

9. My twin brother, *Greg*, is very proud of his partner, *Martin*.

    Both nouns are nonrestrictive, so they should be set apart with commas. Presumably, the writer of the sentence is referring to his one and only twin, and presumably, that brother has only one partner.

10. In the view of the small-town newspaper editor, *James Borred*, the 12-foot worm was nothing to get excited about.

    The phrase is nonrestrictive, so it should be enclosed in commas.

Section 43f (2)

1. No change required [The commas could be added if there were no other women at the location where the documents were to be delivered.]

2. My friend Paul, who was sending me postcards all summer, is the only person I know who has been to Nigeria. [The commas would be omitted if the person had more than one friend named Paul and the context of this sentence made it possible to confuse the two.]

3. The French army, with hopes of fortifying its last remaining stronghold, retreated behind the city walls. [Omitting the commas would be unlikely, but possible: If there was more than one French army—one with hopes, (an) other(s) without hopes—the commas would be necessary.]

4. Bonsai trees, which require great attention and patience, are not naturally so small. [Here the commas are necessary because, regardless of their maintenance requirements, all bonsai trees are artificially small.]

5. The president of the company, David, is the only person who can make that decision.

6. The left winger, a recent addition to the team, has already scored a team-leading twelve goals this season.

7. Leena, who has an interest in computers, wants to get a diploma in graphic design. [The commas would only be omitted if there were two people named Leena being discussed in the context of this sentence.]

8. One of McLuhan's most quoted books, *Understanding Media*, was published in 1964.

9. No change required

10. Vancouver's First Narrows Bridge, better known as the Lions Gate Bridge, connects the downtown area to the north shore.

Section 43 (1)

1. Others, such as political activists, may be arrested several times for their activities, yet they continue to protest.

2. The stories they tell, the characters they portray, and the stereotypes they convey shape and reflect our popular culture.

3. His wife, Candice, believed children should be introduced to different types of music.

4. Despite the controversies, and despite the passions they usually unleash, rights and freedoms have had a low profile in Canadian politics for most of this country's history.

5. The second graph, on the other hand, indicates some of the consequences of providing informal care to an older person.

6. Correct.

7. Amal is captain of the hockey team, and he is also a graceful, athletic figure skater.
8. Mobile communications have made it possible for employees to be part of virtual project teams, which can eliminate time and space barriers and still provide quality, low-cost solutions to organizational problems.

Sections 43 (2)

1. Katie, who seems to excel at any sport she tries, has also signed up for the water-polo team.
2. My roommate wrote a poem, and it was published in the college's only literary journal, *Stanza*.
3. The evidence in the second article, however, is much more damning.
4. Elm, Maple, and Beech trees lined the main street in Woodstock, Ontario.
5. Gaston is taking introductory French, but his teacher, Madame Denis, suspects he should be in the other class that she teaches, which meets on Monday.
6. A new department at the university, Nanotechnology will attract more students, inspire new research, and enlarge the engineering faculty.
7. Rasheed, will you at least help us put up one of the tents or a tarpaulin?
8. Failing to anticipate the volume of sales, the company quickly ran out of inventory.
9. I missed on my first attempt, but I tried again after being encouraged by Thomas, one of the other competitors.
10. The women distributed pamphlets to all who passed by, even those who initially refused, and half the town had read their manifesto by the end of the day.
11. No punctuation required.
12. My friend Kayleigh is travelling to Moose Jaw, Saskatchewan, because her father lives there, and she has not seen him in a very long time.

Section 44

1. I am not sure, but I think I'm in the wrong tutorial; I will find out tomorrow.
2. Some people may see an area of wetland as a valuable scientific or recreational landscape; others will see it as potential farm or building land.
3. Besides the immediate recipients of your expense report, there may be several other readers, including your supervisor, the financial controller of the company, or a budget committee.
4. One group claims that travel and tourism account for about $5.9 trillion of economic activity, which is about 10 per cent of global GDP.
5. Dictionaries also have entries for phrases, including idioms; look under the main word in the expression.
6. Firefighters had the trust of 97 per cent of Canadians in 2012; nurses, 94 per cent; teachers, 89 per cent; and police officers, 84 per cent.
7. The imaginative work of the reader, however, remains the same for historical fiction as for fantasy.
8. The opening paragraph introduces not only the essay but also its writer; therefore, you must appear credible and reliable.
9. Even the dead of this city cannot rest in peace; their bones are dug up by desperate children and sold to bone-dealers.

Section 43–45

1. Everyone thought the technological revolution would reduce our use of paper; we were wrong.
2. Jamil needed some help with his lab report, so he thought he would make an appointment with a tutor.
3. Cartoons are enjoyed by both children and adults; sometimes adults enjoy them more.
4. Some people eat to live; others live to eat. **OR** Some people eat to live, others live to eat.
5. It was a fascinating hypothesis, but it was greeted with silence.
6. His belly shook, he had a red nose, he was surrounded by reindeer.

   OR

   His belly shook; he had a red nose; he was surrounded by reindeer.
7. The hurricane warning went up, and most people sauntered to their shelters; others continued to watch TV.
8. Easy come, easy go. **OR** Easy come; easy go.
9. You live, you learn. **OR** You live; you learn.
10. The strike was over; the people were jubilant.

Section 44–46

1. Appropriate
2. Appropriate
3. Inappropriate. We left the market, and after driving for fifteen minutes, we arrived home with our groceries.
4. Inappropriate. Who should own the Rosetta Stone? Should it be the English?
5. Inappropriate. The next time they do something like this, bring out the fire trucks and hose them all down.
6. Appropriate
7. Inappropriate. Mario got a speeding ticket, told a lie, and dug himself in deeper.
8. Appropriate
9. Appropriate
10. Inappropriate. Please call our booking agency—Funambulists Incorporated—about hiring us for your next event.

Section 43g, 46, 47

1. It was seven o'clock in the evening—a mild autumn evening—and the crickets were beginning to chirp.
2. No one (at least no one who was present) wanted to disagree with the speaker's position.
3. Early one Sunday morning—a morning I will never forget—the phone rang unexpectedly.
4. Since it was only a mild interjection (no more than a barely audible snort from the back of the room) he went on with scarcely a pause, but with a slightly raised eyebrow, and finished his speech.
5. And then suddenly, out of the blue and into my head, came the only possible answer.

Sections 54a–b (also 33–34) (1)

1. I had not been back in ages; therefore, I was surprised to see all the changes.

2. We started to edit the next edition of the newsletter; soon the office was littered with coffee cups and paper.

3. Atwood uses figurative language; however, the literal sense is sufficiently clear.

4. But we sat silent: the scene before us on the stage had left us stunned.

5. No change needed

6. This sales letter doesn't acknowledge women exist; therefore, they will never buy the product.

7. No change needed

8. The dictator's statue stood for almost thirty years; however, it was toppled in less than an hour.

9. We pushed off from the shore; the canoes were buffeted by the waves; we found ourselves unexpectedly in the water.

10. Things went suspiciously well: the first person who looked at the house wanted to buy it.

Sections 54a–b (also 33–34) (2)

1. (run-on) Ann-Marie MacDonald is well known as a novelist. She also writes plays.

2. (comma splice) Alison needed visuals for her poster. However, only maps of other areas were available.

3. Correct.

4. (comma splice) The mechanics, although they started late, have promised to finish the job. They will get your car back on the road.

5. (run-on) We knew the solution, already very potent, would get even stronger if we added the crystals, so we poured them in.

6. Correct.

7. (run-on) Known for her fairness, the bank manager promised her staff raises or improvement of their benefits.

8. (run-on) They looked angry when they arrived, so we packed up and left, disappointed to give up the field.

9. (comma splice) The trumpet player took a solo, the band behind him sounding amazing.

10. (run-on) Because frogs breathe partially through their skin, they are sensitive to pollution; they also indicate environmental health.

Sections 54a–b (also 33–34) (3)

(1) (comma splice) Many Canadians have heard Roberta Bondar's name. **Some** of us might know she was an astronaut, but we do not know anything else about her.

(3) (comma splice) She was Canada's first female astronaut; additionally, she was the first neurologist in space.

(5) (run-on) She has not been in space the whole time, but her research for over a decade has examined the way astronauts recover from the microgravity of space.

(7) (comma splice) **Although** Bondar's achievements in space are many, she has also been very busy on Earth.

(8) (run on) She is a passionate environmentalist, and she has worked hard to inform and advise individuals, companies, and governments. **Improving** environmental education in secondary and elementary schools has been one of her biggest efforts.

(9) (comma splice) She is also an author, public speaker, acclaimed photographer, and until 2009, she was the chancellor of Trent University in Ontario. **What** an incredible woman!

Sections 43–46

1. The first stanza describes a series of seemingly unconnected items: a pair of sandals, a ship's hull, a wooden dresser, and twenty-five truffles.

2. L.M. Montgomery's novel *The Story Girl* is my favourite book; however, *Anne of Green Gables* also has a special place in my heart.

3. Social rituals, such as funerals and marriages, are important; they create cohesion.

4. Rahiq, having discovered the source of the problem, immediately started thinking of solutions.

5. She walked through the hallway, pausing to admire the artwork on the walls.

6. When Susan returned it to her, the pashmina scarf—the precious gift that her sister had brought back for her all the way from Kathmandu—was ripped. [Commas could also be used here.]

7. Zacharias Kunuk worked for the Inuit Broadcasting Corporation, started his own production company, and released several documentaries and short dramas; but his most recognized achievement was his full-length movie, *Atanarjuat.*

8. His mother, who went to university in Pakistan before coming to Canada, is a professor of pure mathematics at the university.

9. Knowing what he did of the owner's character, he could only see one motive driving the recent round of layoffs: greed.

10. No punctuation necessary.

Section 52

1. . . . the young woman said, "I only enjoy watching basketball, soccer, and tennis."

2. The instructor warned her students, "I don't want to hear a single electronic beep."

3. "What about my BlackBerry?" asked Larry. "Does it count?"

4. Hamlet's most recognized soliloquy begins "to be or not to be."

5. Roberta said, "Juliet claims that she wasn't there."

6. Macdonald's discontent is evident in his journals: "The progress of this government is slow and nearly intolerable."

7. Two notable examples of hockey in Canadian literature are Michael Ondaatje's poem "To a Sad Daughter" and Wayne Johnston's short story collection *Original Six.*

8. We later found out that our professor's "field research excursions" were actually week-long drinking benders. [Commas are optional here depending on the tone intended by the author.]

9. "The new hospitals will be built after 2011," replied the government's spokesperson.

10. "Has no one here read Dorothy Livesay's poem 'The Three Emilys'?" asked the poetry society president exasperatedly.

11. No quotation marks required.

Sections 43–54 (1)

Lake Winnipeg is the tenth-largest freshwater lake in the world. Even more impressive, its watershed is the second largest in Canada and includes large areas of four provinces (Ontario, Manitoba, Alberta, and Saskatchewan) and two states (North Dakota and Minnesota). A rapid rate of replenishment and a shallow depth—the average for the entire lake is only 12 metres—make the lake especially habitable for fish. The lake helps to make Manitoba the second-largest freshwater fishery in Canada, and its abundance of walleye, a popular sport fish, brings thousands of anglers to the lake every year. In fact, Lake Winnipeg is one of Manitoba's primary recreational resources, attracting not just anglers, but tourists, who come for the natural beauty of the lake and the excellent boating, hiking, cycling, and camping that it offers.

In recent years, concern about the ecological health of the lake has increased. Surprisingly, the biggest threat is a naturally occurring plant: blue-green algae. The overgrowth of this plant, which is extremely harmful to ecosystems, is the result of human practices within the watershed. Agricultural runoff and sewage from cities and towns flow into the lake, eventually overloading the lake water with phosphorus and nitrogen. These two elements act as fertilizer and create unnaturally large algae blooms, which deplete the oxygen that the lake's ecosystem needs to function naturally. The blooms can devastate a fish population. Additionally, they are toxic and can force the closure of beaches to people. Because of the importance of the fishery and tourism to the Manitoba economy, the government is starting to work to protect the lake; however, it must act quickly and before it is too late.

Sections 43–54 (2)

Some people ask, "who were Canada's Famous Five?" They were five women from Alberta who changed the political life of women in Canada: Emily Murphy, a social activist; Nellie McClung, a novelist and journalist; Louise McKinney, a politician; Irene Parlby, also a politician; and Henrietta Muir Edwards, a journalist. They were all involved in women's suffrage, but their most widely recognized achievement came in the late 1920s through what is know as the "Persons" Case. The efforts of these five women in the case, which took place between 1927 and 1929, resulted in women gaining the legal ability to sit in the Senate.

The reason it became known as the "Persons" Case was its focus on use of the word in section twenty-four of *The British North America Act,* which refers to the "persons" eligible to sit in the Senate. The Famous Five took the bold step of asking the Supreme Court of Canada to clarify the document. It may seem odd—at least to most "persons" today—that this was even something that required clarification. However, in its initial 1927 ruling, the Court rejected the idea that "persons" included women. It said that *The BNA Act* was drafted in 1867 when women did not hold political office; therefore, when its authors wrote "persons," they meant "men." The Famous Five were not satisfied with this response and appealed the decision to the highest court of appeal possible, the Judicial Committee of England's Privy Council. Their appeal was successful, the Judicial Committee ruling unanimously that women were allowed to hold seats in the senate.

Although none of the Famous Five ever became senators, the first female senator, Cairine Wilson, was admitted to the Canadian Senate only four months after the Five's successful appeal. In 2013, there were over thirty female members of the senate. The work of the Famous Five was an important early step in the struggle for equality, and their efforts continue to inspire people who seek equal social, economic, and political rights today. Recently, a monument on Parliament Hill in Ottawa, Ontario, was erected to commemorate their contribution to the lives of all Canadians.

Review exercises: Part V

A. CORRECTING PUNCTUATION

1. Rainer Maria Rilke says, "love occurs when two solitudes protect and touch and greet each other."

2. I believe that, for a number of reasons, genetically modified food should be carefully regulated.

3. He was not a frightening poltergeist but an irritating one; he hid the remote control and moved the coffee table.

4. Many of his plays are about royalty, as in the Lancastrian tetralogy *Richard II*, *Henry IV (1)*, *Henry IV (2)*, and *Henry V*.

5. His childlike features were deceptive, as we discovered when the alien from the planet Zotar began to give us detailed instructions on how to build a time machine.

6. When you spend time with close friends, you get a different perspective: life seems less narrow and serious.

7. With him, too, she felt comfortable.

8. I would like to wake up in the morning—especially a beautiful morning such as this—and not feel the burden of work.

9. The encounter that deepened his feelings more occurred at age nine. [The comma after *more* has been removed as it is a comma fault.]

10. Therefore, one must always remember to be polite when encountering a ghostly stranger in a train station.

11. This, then, was the plan: return to our campsite for the night, and tackle Black Tusk the next morning.

12. I joined in—dancing haltingly at first and then more confidently.

13. As a person exercises, the muscle of the heart becomes stronger; therefore, it can pump more blood while beating less.

14. However, I always wake up the next day with the worst sort of headache—the emotional headache.

15. The meal started with grilled artichokes followed by mushroom ravioli, and finished with a lemon tart.

16. It was, after all, exactly what he had asked for.

17. Crisp memories of laughing eyes, loving smiles, and peaceful, easy feelings still linger.

18. A computer hard drive is easy to install: just remember to ground yourself before you touch the hard drive.

19. Did Sheila Watson write *The Double Hook*?

20. Eighteenth-century mathematicians, unlike their counterparts in the seventeenth century, were able to develop both pure and applied mathematics. Leonhard Euler, a notable genius in both these fields, contributed invaluably to every branch of mathematics.

21. Another classic film that explores the effects of war on individual lives is *Casablanca*. [The commas appearing around the *that*-clause have been removed, as the clause is restrictive and should not be set apart with punctuation.]

22. It began to rain; nevertheless, since they were on the sixteenth fairway, they went ahead and finished the round.

23. When the tyrant stood up and said "you rascals, you will get what you deserve," a brick fell on his head.

24. To me, this indicates that although he remembers the details of the events he describes,

there is an enormous space of time—between them **(the events)** and the present—that makes **the details** intangible.

25. The sounds of the sonata are soft and never harsh, which helps create the melancholy mood.

B. USING PUNCTUATION

1. When the meeting ended, he went to a pub for a drink.

2. Doggedly, Peyvand finished his essay.

3. Soon, **[optional comma]** those parts became unappealing, and she decided to fire her current agent.

4. In 2000, he moved to Halifax, Nova Scotia, and bought a small, reputable art gallery specializing in expensive, striking, white, minimalist plastic sculpture.

5. She felt uneasy about the trip, yet she knew she had to go and meet her sister flying in from Hong Kong.

6. I took the book that I didn't like back to the library, but I still had to pay a fine.

7. Mary, Winnie, and Cora came to the party together but left separately.

8. He had a broad, engaging smile, **[optional comma]** even though he had three teeth missing.

9. Having heard all she wanted, Bridget walked out of the meeting.

10. But once you've taken the first few steps, the rest will naturally be easy.

11. The poem was short; the novel was long; the poem was good, the novel better.

12. No punctuation needed

13. But Canadians don't think that way: they prefer to sit back and wait. [In place of the colon added here, a semicolon could also be used.]

14. Last summer, **[optional comma]** we visited Hastings, the site of the battle won by William the Conqueror in 1066.

15. A warm bath, a good book, and freshly laundered sheets were all she wanted.

16. There are only three vegetables I can't tolerate: turnips, turnips, and turnips.

17. In the good old days, the doctor, a specialist in family practice, made house calls all morning.

18. August 16, 1977, is when Elvis Presley died.

19. He had to finish the novel quickly, or he wouldn't get his advance.

20. We arrived, we ate, we partook in boring conversation; we departed, and that's all there was to the evening.

21. You must plan your budget carefully in times of inflation, so remember to buy lottery tickets.

22. She is the only woman I know who wears pantyhose every day, **[optional comma]** whatever the season.

23. His several hobbies were philately, woodworking, chess, and fishing.

24. The two opponents settled the question amicably at the meeting, **[optional comma]** and then went home to write nasty letters to each other and to the editor of the local newspaper.

25. He would rather make up a lie than stick to the boring truth: that was his downfall.

Part VI
Mechanics and Spelling

Using abbreviations correctly
pp. 284–287

Correct each sentence to eliminate all errors and all abbreviations that would be inappropriate in formal writing.

1. Gordon Reid MD travelled down the road toward his family's cottage in Normans Cove, Nfld.

2. Several members of C.U.P.E. are planning to strike next wed.

3. When you get to the end of 14th ave., turn right (i.e., west).

4. Governor Gen. David Johnston will hand out the awards at 8:30 PM.

5. I earned my PH.D from U British Columbia in 2004 and was teaching English lit. soon after.

6. The nrc employs almost 4,000 people working in dozens of industries (ie. aerospace, biotechnology, manufacturing, etc.)

Capitalization, titles, and italics
pp. 287–298

Identify and correct all errors involving capitalization, italics, and the treatment of titles in the following sentences. If the sentence is correct place a check mark beside it.

1. You should learn the distinction between *disinterested* and uninterested.

2. A little further down Maple street you will pass the Anglican Church.

3. In Joseph Conrad's novel Lord Jim, the main character begins as Chief Mate on board the Patna.

4. The Leader of The Wildrose Party, Danielle Smith, ascended to power quickly.

5. In Archibald Lampman's poem *The Railway Station*, the speaker is critical of Nineteenth-century industrialism.

6. Professor Patricia Alban received her MA. from Concordia university in montreal.

7. A recent article in my favourite magazine, The walrus, goes into detail about Madam Chief Justice Beverley McLachlin.

8. The company president and I had to get to our meeting in Hootalinqua, Yukon Territory, on a Ski-Doo.

9. My Aunt watches *Hockey night in Canada* religiously.

10. Because our community centre is hosting a visit from the Hon. Peter Mackay, please note that all saturday programs are cancelled.

Using hyphens
pp. 318–321

Insert hyphens wherever they are needed in the following sentences and correct any instances of their misuse. Consult your dictionary if necessary. If the sentence is correct place a check mark beside it.

1. Your schedule is filled with far too many first and second-year courses.

2. Laetitia was looking forward to seeing the fine art museum's collection of eighteenth century paintings.

3. The author was particularly well known for his use of one-syllable words.

4. Thirty three posts were published from August 20-September 2.

5. Forcing the non religious to ascribe to a form of organized religion is not only un productive, it is also un Canadian.

6. Three-fourths of the flour needs to be saved for the end of the recipe.

7. The premier elect decided that her first action would be a reduction in small business taxation.

8. French speaking people were less likely to misinterpret the deliberately-confusing sign.

9. Greek word-formation still influences the way we spell words in modern-times.

10. Tanya's dress was lily-of-the-valley white.

Using hyphens

pp. 318–321

Insert hyphens wherever they are needed in the following sentences. Consult your dictionary if necessary.

1. The ferry is thirty two and one quarter metres long.

2. The all Canadian team proved too much even for the ex champions.

3. The cold hearted vice president took up motor racing instead of profit sharing.

4. Is that an old fashioned and beautifully made antique salt cellar I see in your china cabinet?

5. The three tough looking youths were set to dish out some abuse.

6. I watched an interesting two hour documentary about improving selfesteem.

7. Avoid the scatter shot approach when writing a complaint email to part time employees.

8. The long lived queen has been a full time ruler from an early age.

Forming plurals

pp. 321–326

Write out what you think is the correct plural form of each of the following nouns, then check your dictionary to see if you are right.

1. aide-de-camp _____

2. alley _____

3. bonus _____

4. broadleaf _____

5. bus _____

6. embargo _____

7. fifth _____

8. fish _____

9. flyby _____

10. gloss _____

11. goose _____

12. handful _____

13. mongoose _____

14. mosquito _____

15. museum _____

16. octopus _____

17. ox _____

18. plateau _____

19. radius _____

20. serf _____

21. society _____

22. solo _____

23. speech _____

24. staff _____

25. territory _____

26. town _____

27. wife _____

28. yellow _____

Using apostrophes

pp. 321–329

Insert apostrophes where necessary in the following sentences.

1. I dont know whether this book is hers, but theres no doubt its a handsome one and its value has increased since the 1930s.

2. Clearly he doesnt know whats going on: itll take him a weeks study to catch up.

3. Our end-of-term reports are ready, but well have to revise them.

4. It isnt the resume that will get you the job but whom you know that will count.

5. Bonnies guess is closer than Jesss, but the jars full and accurate count of beans wont be verified till Monday.

6. The professors comments about Richs paper pointed out its errors.

7. I have two years experience in working with apostrophe problems.

8. It doesnt matter whether one wins or loses but how one plays the game.

9. When all the cars alarms started, the Joneses neighbours had to shut their windows.

10. The Canadians approach to traffic is to stop for Canada geese and other passersby.

Using apostrophes

pp. 321–329

In the following sentences, supply any missing apostrophes and correct any instances of their misuse and any associated errors.

1.   Childrens toys are often made in countrys where the children do not play because theyre working.

2.   He was taken aback by the spectacle of the St. Vituss Dance.

3.   The two main characters are each others foils.

4.   He acted without a moments hesitation.

5.   We will meet again in three weeks time.

6.   Have you read Herman Hesss *The Glass Bead Game*?

7.   If its to perform it's duties properly, the committees agenda needs to undergo numerous changes.

8.   You can buy boys and girls swim suits in many of the local malls shops.

9.   The Haris' came to dinner.

10.   When someone misuse's apostrophes's, it shows they don't understand the rules'.

Correcting misspellings

pp. 330–334

Underline the misspelled words in the following sentences and provide a correction. Add any words you miss to a list for future practice.

paraphernalia

Example: If I find any drug <u>peraphernalia</u> in your dorm room, I will call the dean.

1. Jeremy, a playright new to the Montreal scene, has just finished a one-act work about the practise of cannibalism.

2. Our professor always expects us to excede his demands, and he is unflinching when it comes to plagiarism.

3. This knowledgeable paper explores the theme of tyrrany in *Richard III.*

4. In the labratory the scientists were innoculating children against Rubella with the new vacine.

5. Take these plates into the dinning room imediately.

6. You will find the acceptible forms in the personel department.

7. The foreign atheletes think our equiptment is wierd.

8. Our grandfather always recalls the mischevous pranks of his childhood with such wistfulness.

9. I advice you to hire the second team so we can put the earlier embarassment behind us.

10. Much to the dismay of the community, the company built its refinery on the land that it pubilcally accquired in 2006.

Revising paragraphs

pp. 281–334

Correct all errors in the following paragraph.

The W.h.o reports that cervical cancer is the second-most-prevalant cancer among women worldwide, and it accounts for nearly 250,000 deaths each year. It's main risk factor is the contraction of the human papilloma virus (HPV). Researchers have developed a HPV vacination to protect against the two most common high-risk stranes (e.g., HPV 16 and 18). In the "Cancer Treatment Journal", Dr Jennifer Shinkoda comments, "the vaccine produces a neutralizing response by creating anti-bodys that aid the prevention of early-viral infection or spread." Because their unlikely to have been exposed to HPV through sexual activity, younger females between the ages of nine- and 26 are the target for the vaccine. Researcher Hiresh Bonjahni, Ph.D., at The Montreal Childrens Hospital has showen that the "prophylactic quadrivalent vaccine is 100% effective" against pre cancerous legions of the servix. Unfortunately, the dureation of protection is unknown, but the early results are promiseing.

Part VI: Answers

Section 56

1. Gordon Reid, **M.D.**, travelled down the road toward his family's cottage in Normans Cove, **Newfoundland.**

2. Several members of **CUPE** are planning to strike next **Wednesday**.

3. When you get to the end of 14th **Avenue**, turn right (i.e., west).

4. **Governor General** David Johnston will hand out the awards at 8:30 **p.m**.

5. I earned my **Ph.D.** from the **University of British Columbia** in 2004 and was teaching English **literature** soon after.

6. The **NRC** employs almost 4,000 people working in dozens of industries (**e.g.,** aerospace, biotechnology, manufacturing).

Sections 57–59

1. You should learn the distinction between *disinterested* and **uninterested**.

2. A little further down Maple **Street** you will pass the Anglican **church**.

3. In Joseph Conrad's novel ***Lord Jim***, the main character begins as chief mate on board the ***Patna***.

4. **The leader** of **the** Wildrose Party, Danielle Smith, ascended to power quickly.

5. In Archibald Lampman's poem **"The Railway Station,"** the speaker is critical of **nineteenth-century** industrialism.

6. Professor Patricia Alban received her **M.A.** from Concordia **University** in **Montreal.**

7. A recent article in my favourite magazine, ***The Walrus***, goes into detail about Madam Chief Justice Beverley McLachlin.

8. Correct.

9. My aunt watches *Hockey Night in Canada* religiously.

10. Because our community centre is hosting a visit from the **Honourable Peter MacKay**, please note that all **Saturday** programs are cancelled.

Section 61k (1)

1. Your schedule is filled with far too many **first-** and second-year courses.

2. Laetitia was looking forward to seeing the fine art museum's collection of **eighteenth-century** paintings.

3. Correct.

4. **Thirty-three** posts were published between August 20 **and** September 2.

5. Forcing the **non-religious** to ascribe to a form of organized religion is not only **unproductive**, it is also **un-Canadian**.

6. Correct.

7. The **premier-elect** decided that her first action would be a reduction in **small-business** taxation.

8. **French-speaking** people were less likely to misinterpret the **deliberately confusing** sign.

9. Greek word-formation still influences the way we spell words in **modern times**.

10. Correct.

Section 61k (2)

1. The ferry is **thirty-two** and **one-quarter** metres long.

2. The **all-Canadian** team proved too much even for the **ex-champions**.

3. The **cold-hearted vice-president** took up motor racing instead of **profit-sharing**.

4. Is that an **old-fashioned** and beautifully made antique salt cellar I see in your china cabinet?

5. The three **tough-looking** youths were set to dish out some abuse.

6. I watched an interesting **two-hour** documentary about improving **self-esteem**.

7. Avoid the **scatter-shot** approach when writing a complaint **e-mail** to **part-time** employees.

8. The **long-lived** queen has been a **full-time** ruler from an early age.

Section 62-l

1. aide-de-camp – aides-de-camp
2. alley – alleys
3. bonus – bonuses
4. broadleaf – broadleaves
5. bus – buses
6. embargo – embargoes
7. fifth – fifths
8. fish – fish or fishes (different species)
9. flyby – flybys
10. gloss – glosses
11. goose – geese
12. handful – handfuls
13. mongoose – mongooses
14. mosquito – mosquitoes
15. museum – museums
16. octopus – octopi
17. ox – oxen
18. plateau – plateaus or plateaux
19. radius – radii
20. serf – serfs
21. society – societies
22. solo – solos
23. speech – speeches
24. staff – staffs or staves
25. territory – territories
26. town – towns
27. wife – wives
28. yellow – yellows

Section 61-l–n (1)

1. I don't know whether this book is hers, but there's no doubt it's a handsome one and its value has increased since the 1930's.

2. Clearly he doesn't know what's going on; it'll take him a week's study to catch up.

3. Our end-of-term reports are ready, but we'll have to revise them.

4. It isn't the resume that will get you the job but whom you know that will count.

5. Bonnie's guess is closer than Jess's, but the jar's full and accurate count of beans won't be verified till Monday.

6. The professor's comments about Rich's paper pointed out its errors.

7. I have two years' experience in working with apostrophe problems.

8. It doesn't matter whether one wins or loses but how one plays the game.

9. When all the cars' alarms started, the Joneses' neighbours had to shut their windows.

10. The Canadian's approach to traffic is to stop for Canada geese and other passersby.

Section 61-l–n (2)

1. Children's toys are often made in count**ries** where the children do not play because they're working.

2. He was taken aback by the spectacle of the St. Vitus's Dance.

3. The two main characters are each other's foils.

4. He acted without a moment's hesitation.

5. We will meet again in three weeks' time.

6. Have you read Herman Hess's *The Glass Bead Game*?

7. If it's to perform **its** duties properly, the committee's agenda needs to undergo numerous changes. [An even clearer sentence would be this one: If the committee is to perform its duties properly, the committee's agenda needs to undergo numerous changes.]

8. You can buy boys' and girls' swim suits in many of the local mall's shops.

9. The Haris came to dinner. [The guests' last name is Hari.]

10. When someone misus**es** apostroph**es**, it shows they don't understand the rul**es**.

Section 62

1. <u>playright</u>, *playwright*; <u>practise</u>, *practice*

2. <u>excede</u>, *exceed*

3. <u>tyrrany</u>, *tyranny*

4. <u>labratory</u>, *laboratory*; <u>innoculating</u>, *inoculating*; <u>vacine</u>, *vaccine*

5. <u>dinning</u>, *dining*; <u>imediately</u>, *immediately*

6. <u>acceptible</u>, *acceptable*; <u>personel</u>, *personnel*

7. <u>atheletes</u>, *athletes*; <u>equiptment</u>, *equipment*; <u>wierd</u>, *weird*

8. <u>mischevous</u>, *mischievous*

9. <u>advice</u>, *advise*; <u>embarassment</u>, *embarrassment*

10. <u>publicly</u>, *publicly*; <u>accquired</u>, *acquired*

Review exercise: Part VI

The **WHO** reports that cervical cancer is the **second most prevalent** cancer among women worldwide, and it accounts for nearly 250,000 deaths each year. **Its** main risk factor is the contraction of the human papilloma virus (HPV). Researchers have developed a HPV **vaccination** to protect against the two most common high-risk **strains (i.e.,** HPV 16 and 18). In the *Cancer Treatment Journal,* Dr. Jennifer Shinkoda comments, "the vaccine produces a neutralizing response by creating **antibodies** that aid the prevention of **early viral** infection or spread." Because **they are** unlikely to have been exposed to HPV through sexual activity, younger females between the ages of **nine** and **twenty-six** are the target for the vaccine. Hiresh Bonjahni, Ph.D., a **researcher** at the Montreal **Children's** Hospital has **shown** that the "prophylactic quadrivalent vaccine is 100% effective" against **precancerous lesions** of the **cervix.** Unfortunately, the **duration** of protection is unknown, but the early results are **promising**.

Part VII
Diction

Using formal diction

pp. 344–346

Provide formal substitutes for each of the slang or informal terms below. Use your dictionary or thesaurus as necessary. Then compose sentences for at least ten of the listed terms, using them in ways that you think would be acceptable in relatively formal writing.

1. cheapskate _____
2. chintzy _____
3. con (v.) _____
4. conniption _____
5. cook up _____
6. crackdown _____
7. dress down _____
8. jock _____
9. cute _____
10. ditch _____
11. down the tube _____
12. face the music _____
13. fall guy _____

14. go downhill _____
15. high and mighty _____
16. hunch _____
17. jerk _____
18. miss out _____
19. on the spot _____
20. scrounge _____
21. slapdash _____
22. southpaw _____
23. egghead _____
24. shocker _____
25. up the creek _____

Slang, colloquialisms, and informal expressions
pp. 344–346

Revise the following sentences to eliminate the unnecessary slang, colloquialisms, and informal words and phrases.

1. Canadians can get a lot out of learning both French and English.

2. Gulliver encounters several random situations including a land full of people way smaller than normal.

3. Sketchy people hang out in the park near my house.

4. At the beginning of *The Taming of the Shrew*, Sly gets wasted, falls asleep, and gets fooled into thinking he is a nobleman.

5. Characters in the book use hilariously dated phrases like "Twern't me McGee" and "Lay some skin on me Flynn."

6. Juliet looks amazing, which inspires Romeo to perform several dicey actions.

7. The results of our cloning experiment were nowhere near what we expected.

8. We need to analyze the policy decisions before we try and develop our plan.

9. The collapse of the market has made selecting stocks way more hard.

10. Mrs. Jellyby's obsession with philanthropy causes her to totally ignore her own kids.

Thinking about "big" words

p. 346–347

For each of the following words, provide one or more equivalents that are less formal and more natural. Use your dictionary or thesaurus as necessary. Which of these words do you recognize but not use yourself? Which do you consider to be in your working vocabulary? Mark any that you consider to be pretentious or overly formal in a non-academic context.

1. ablutions _____
2. assiduity _____
3. bellicose _____
4. cachinnation _____
5. circumambient _____
6. collation _____
7. colloquy _____
8. comminatory _____
9. compotation _____
10. concatenation _____
11. confabulate _____
12. conflagration _____
13. contumelious _____
14. crepuscular _____
15. defenestration _____
16. divagation _____
17. doff _____
18. egress _____
19. eleemosynary _____
20. equitation _____
21. erstwhile _____
22. frangible _____
23. gustatory _____
24. habiliments _____
25. hebdomadal _____
26. impudicity _____
27. ineluctable _____
28. jejune _____

29. lubricity _____
30. lucubrations _____
31. matutinal _____
32. mentation _____
33. objurgation _____
34. obloquy _____
35. oppugning _____
36. orthography _____
37. otiose _____
38. pellucid _____
39. penurious _____
40. peregrinations _____
41. propinquity _____
42. raison d'être _____
43. rebarbative _____
44. repast _____
45. rubicund _____
46. salubrious _____
47. sartorial _____
48. serendipitous _____
49. sesquipedalian _____
50. superincumbent _____
51. tenebrous _____
52. transpontine _____
53. vilipend _____
54. visage _____
55. veridical _____
56. Weltanschauung _____

Eliminating pretentious diction

p. 346–347

Using a dictionary if necessary, express the following in less pretentious diction.

1. Donald defenestrated his microcomputer.

2. Fortuitously, Sri was able to acquire the two concert tickets for which he was pining.

3. Individuals who inhabit vitreous abodes should refrain from propelling lapidary projectiles.

4. Our pedagogue disseminated the examinations and verbally prohibited us from confabulation.

5. The prototype has drastically transmogrified from our initial adumbrations.

Using specific diction

pp. 350–354

For each of the following words, supply several increasingly specific terms; take at least a few all the way to a single specific item.

1.	car	**10.**	entertainment
2.	art	**11.**	creature
3.	answered	**12.**	structure
4.	said	**13.**	see
5.	food	**14.**	moved
6.	drink (v.)	**15.**	concept
7.	drink (n.)	**16.**	freedom
8.	people	**17.**	music
9.	mythical thing		

Next, compose a paragraph in which you use one or two of these seventeen general terms in the first sentence and develop your idea by using increasingly specific terms.

Being concrete and specific
pp. 350–354

Rewrite the following vague and abstract paragraph from a letter of application for an entry-level research position at a community newspaper. The ad for the position called for details of the applicant's educational and employment experience, so in your revision, try to make the paragraph sharp and vivid by supplying concrete and specific details wherever suitable.

My education and job experience make me a good person to work in your organization. At university, I have been studying courses in arts and science, and I have done quite a bit of research and writing of various things along the way. I have worked as a volunteer in my community, and over the years, I have been employed in three jobs that have given me good experience working in a busy office setting.

Recognizing connotation
pp. 354–355

Label each of the following words as having an unfavourable (u), neutral (n), or favourable (f) connotation; it might help if you place the words in each group on a scale running from u to f. Explain cases where you think some could be labelled more than one way, depending on context. Use your dictionary if necessary.

1. artless crass dense dull dumb feeble-minded foolish green ignorant inept ingenuous innocent naïve obtuse shallow simple slow stupid thick unsophisticated unthinking

2. bony gaunt lanky lean rawboned scrawny skinny slender slight slim spare spindly svelte thin trim twiggy underweight weedy

3. artful clever crafty cunning devious diplomatic foxy greasy guileful insinuating oily scheming slimy slippery sly smooth suave tricky unctuous wily

4. arrogance assurance audacity boldness brass brazenness cheek chutzpah effrontery gall highhandedness impertinence impudence insolence nerve pride presumption temerity

5. bookworm brain brainworker egghead genius highbrow intellectual mind pedant pundit sage savant scholar smarty thinker geek

Section 68

Avoiding euphemisms
pp. 355–356

Supply more straightforward equivalents for the following terms.

1. job action, work stoppage _____

2. revenue enhancement _____

3. repeat offender _____

4. correctional facility _____

5. underprivileged, deprived, disadvantaged _____

6. surveillance satellites _____

7. in custody _____

8. memorial chapel; memorial park _____

9. untruth _____

10. friendly fire _____

11. indisposed _____

12. weather event _____

Avoiding wrong words

p. 356–357

Correct the wrong words in the following sentences.

1. It was an incredulous display of manual dexterity.

2. The Office of the Auditor General, who is an independent office of the Legislative Assembly, conducts audits.

3. The company's representatives claimed to be authoritarians on the subject.

4. The performance of our local orchestra was spirited and bombastic.

5. We tried to convince her that her fear was entirely imaginative.

6. Some shoppers stopped buying coffee because they found the price so absorbent, if not gastronomical.

7. The premier of Alberta led his party to the best of his possibilities.

8. He was deciduously on the wrong track with his research.

9. The conference is intended to focus attention on the problems facing our effluent society.

10. The cat was very expansive, weighing over twenty pounds.

Avoiding wrong words

p. 356–357

Identify the wrong words in the following sentences and provide a correction.

1. This Winston Churchill biography describes the context for several of his most famous quotes.

2. Being an expatriate in this city carries a certain cache.

3. He was disinterested in the side-effects of the experimental treatment.

4. The prince was very complementary of his subjects' efforts.

5. Philanthropy is a central tenant of his philosophy.

6. The negative affects of high inflation rates were quickly seen in the economy.

7. We were amazed by each of the magician's illusions accept for the last one.

8. The lawyer's conscious prevented her from agreeing to prosecute the case.

9. The imminent philosopher has been awarded another honourary doctorate.

10. Kevin was the passed president of the university's English society.

Correcting idioms

pp. 357–359

Correct the unidiomatic usages in the following sentences.

1. The generation gap between them is evident by their uneasiness of each other's boredom.

2. Tanya made us to laugh with stories of her adventures in the Yukon.

3. Last summer I was bestowed with a scrawny, mangy mutt.

4. Desdemona had unquestioning faith of Iago's character.

5. He suggested me to use this new product.

6. The analysis is weak because it lacks in specific details.

7. I am amazed with the report's suggestions.

8. Lovers and poets create dream worlds in which only they can inhabit.

9. Ironically, although Huck fails, Tom succeeds to free Jim.

10. She has an unusual philosophy towards modern technology.

11. We discussed about global warming.

12. The class emphasized on mathematics skills.

Correcting idioms

pp. 357–359

Correct the unidiomatic usages in the following sentences.

1. New recruits are trained to conform with the values, code of conduct, and dress of the armed forces.

2. During the garage sale, Alfonso reluctantly parted from his beloved television.

3. The imam was prohibited, by the oppressive laws of the state, to address the crowd of his followers.

4. After the thirteen-year-old received his music scholarship he was entrusted in the care of the academy guardians.

5. The new president's directives are no different than his predecessor's.

6. Make sure the new air conditioner that is purchased for the office complies to the rules about energy use.

7. Our study will provide us with insight about how the lack of green spaces in a city can affect residents.

8. Because of his failure to register on time, Pancho was disqualified for competing in the javelin event.

9. When they were deciding the format of the debate, Caroline and Hana agreed with the theme that Bruce suggested.

10. The new regulations about final examinations are definitely cause of complaint.

Cutting redundancy
p. 361–362

Revise the following sentences to eliminate redundancy.

1. She told him in exact and precise terms just what she thought of him.

2. Golding's *Lord of the Flies* concerns a group of young children, all boys, who revert back to savagery.

3. Looking ahead into the future, the economist sees even less rapid growth in Canada's national economy.

4. She approached the door with feelings of fear and dread.

5. He is adventurous in that he likes a challenge and is willing to try new experiences, but he is not adventurous to the point of insanity, though.

6. If one doesn't thoroughly examine every part of the subject fully, one is almost sure to miss something that could be vitally important.

7. Most people would rather flee away from danger than face it squarely.

8. Carol soon realized that she had to make a careful outline first, before she could expect an essay to be well organized.

9. If enough food cannot be supplied for all the people in the world, humankind will have to deal with hunger, starvation, and widespread famine.

10. The singer in the film does not fit the stereotyped image of a musician.

Reducing wordiness
pp. 359–362

Revise the following sentences to eliminate wordiness.

1. Nature is a very strong, powerful image in this poem.

2. The courses being offered today require much more research and thought rather than the age-old memory work that used to plague the education system not too long a time ago.

3. These were the very things that caused him his puzzlement and his bafflement.

4. Advances in developments of modern information technology greatly contribute to making the equipment necessary for computerization of machinery more and more feasible for potential users.

5. Since he has both positive and negative qualities of human nature, Othello is far from perfect and has many faults.

6. Her confidence in expressing her views caused her to develop her faith in herself, which added to her visible strength.

7. The president and the prime minister both shared that view of the foreseeable future.

8. Another device used by the playwright was one of repetition.

9. There were two hundred people outside the auditorium, pressing against the ropes.

10. In the past six months I have been subjected to moving from two locations to other surroundings.

Reducing wordiness by combining sentences
pp. 359–362

Often one can save many words by combining two or more drafted sentences. Try doing that with each of the following excerpts, from students' drafts; cut all the wordiness you can while you're at it.

1. Also, parents who wish to see a game live but do not want to be disturbed by their children have no choice except to leave them attended at home. In this case, the parents would have to hire a babysitter. As a result, the parents end up paying the babysitter as well as for the game.

2. At soccer practice, our coach would single out the players who had the least team spirit. An example of this would be the passing drills in practices. The players who lagged behind on the field would be asked to run laps after practice.

3. There are a surprising number of lawyers and stockbrokers playing the game. This may be because these people must thrive on strategic planning to be in those professions in the first place.

Reducing wordiness, redundancy, and ready-made phrases
pp. 359–363

Revise the following paragraph to eliminate unnecessary wordiness and redundancy.

At this current point in time, I come before you to tell you to cast your vote for me for president in the upcoming student council election tomorrow! There are quite a few reasons why you would be making the right choice. The first reason you would be making the right choice is that I have actual experience being in charge of managing an organization. This fact is evident in my participation as president of the French society last year. Last year, I was also the president of the Amateur Entomologist Association. The second reason you would be making the right choice is because I have already had a chance to negotiate with the school's administration to create positive changes on campus. As a consequence of my various efforts on the green panel, there are new recycling bins that have been installed all over campus. The third reason you would be making the right choice is my school spirit. This is the most important reason. There is not one person who loves this school more than I do. And in the future I will work without stopping to make this the best year we have ever had.

Eliminating clichés
pp. 363–365

Revise the following sentences to eliminate clichés.

be responsible for

Example: The horticultural society will ~~shoulder the burden of~~ planting flowers in
the newly installed beds on Portage Ave.

1. The new business kept Debora as busy as a bee.

2. We began working on the server errors at the crack of dawn.

3. His campaign suffered a crushing blow when reporters caught him taking
bribes.

4. The Spartans fought tooth and nail to hold back the Persians at Thermopylae.

5. The extruded polymer is as flat as a pancake.

6. The infection made him sick as a dog.

7. There is no magic bullet that will solve this city's problems.

8. Hui-Ying turned green with envy when she saw Jehona arrive with Mikhail.

9. Ellisabet's success at the blackjack table was only a flash in the pan.

10. Needless to say, we need to nip the online fraud problem in the bud.

Evaluating nouns used as adjectives

pp. 367

Evaluate the following phrases in which nouns are used as adjectives. Are some unacceptable? If so, what alternatives can you suggest? Would some be acceptable only in certain contexts? Comment on them in other ways if you wish.

1.	task fragmentation	12.	labour force
2.	worker injuries	13.	regime change
3.	child poverty	14.	safety aspects
4.	computer system	15.	department manager
5.	information technology	16.	fear factor
6.	job description	17.	work schedule
7.	resource planning	18.	profit outlook
8.	customer satisfaction	19.	overkill situation
9.	customer billing	20.	clean-up crew
10.	customer complaints	21.	file server
11.	staff organization	22.	face time

Usage

pp. 370–394

Consider all of the following examples to be extracts from formal writing and correct any errors in usage.

1. The amount of H1N1 flu cases seemed to decrease in the second week.

2. The reason why I am contacting you is because your payment is overdue.

3. The international community has made several diplomatic efforts to resolve the tensions between Liberia, Sierra Leone, and Guinea.

4. Whenever we discuss the problems in our relationship, you seem completely disinterested in anything I have to say.

5. The new policies should of prevented policemen from making these types of errors.

6. The new advertising campaign was much more unique than the one that he originally proposed.

7. There's little we can do, and the murderer was already hung anyways.

8. After two sleepless nights, Marissa literally fought with her eyes to keep them from closing.

Sentence revisions
pp. 337–394

Revise the following sentences to strengthen the diction and normalize the usage; correct any other errors you find, as well.

Conserving electricity in your home is a snap and will end up saving you cash by resulting in reduced energy bills. The reduction of your environmental impact is another benefit of conserving electricity. One place to start conserving is with lighting. A facile primary step is replacing the incandescent bulbs in your home to compact fluorescent. Up to 75% less energy is used by these more efficient bulbs and they will make a humungous difference over the course of the year. There is another place to look for potential energy savings and it is heating and cooling. The first step is simple: utilize less. In summer, set your air conditioner to a lower setting—or deactivate it all together and use a fan instead. In winter, wear an additional stratum of clothing and set the temperature lower. There are also other ways that make your heating and cooling more efficient. One of these ways is replacing your furnace and air conditioner filters every season. Another of these ways is using curtains or blinds or drapes to block the sun in the summer months and retain the heat inside in the winter months. You can also save energy by using consumer electronics more efficiently. For example, many devices such as televisions, stereos, and microwaves suck up amounts of electricity even when they are turned "off." Unplugging them when they are not in use can save a surprising amount of juice. These are only a few of the easy steps you can take to save electricity around your home. You will be surprised by how quickly small steps add up and you start saving money!

Diction

pp. 337–394

Revise the following sentences to strengthen the diction and normalize the usage; correct any other errors you find, as well.

1. They discussed the role of the psychiatrist in athlete motivation.

2. The team comprises a close-knit unit that functions on a collective basis.

3. Strategy-wise, we want to position union members in an advantageous situation.

4. Because this particular word occurs frequently throughout the course of the play, it achieves a certain importance.

5. In the winter even less tourist dollars are spent.

6. Her striving to be a perfectionist was evident in her business.

7. Hopefully, this weekend's events will turn out to be successful.

8. He was ignorant as to the proper use of the tools.

9. As is so often the case, one type of error leads to another.

10. This passage is a very essential one in the novel.

11. His metaphors really bring out a sinister feeling which one feels while reading it.

12. Eliot sees his poetry as occupying a kind of niche in a long conveyer belt of accumulated knowledge and poetry.

13. She has him literally at her beckon call.

14. He found himself in a powerless situation.

15. I resolved to do my best in terms of making friends and working hard.

16. The hulls of the tankers were ripped open in a majority of cases, dumping countless barrels of oil into the sea.

17. Hamlet spends the whole play trying to reach a situation where he can revenge his father's death.

18. This poem is concerned with the fact that one should grasp an opportunity quickly.

19. He is only in town on a once-in-a-while basis.

20. The prime minister is waiting for the premiers to show their bottom lines.

21. As she gave me so much money I thanked her profusely.

22. The deal may not have gone ahead if Anderson hadn't been so patient and persistent.

23. People in watching these shows or movies may develop a love for violence as a result of watching this type of program.

24. This man thought it was incumbent upon him to extract revenge.

25. In Olympic sports nationalism is increasingly becoming a more important factor.

26. She saw that this was the last remaining remnant of a very, very important species.

27. For more than a million Canadians, back pain is an incapacitating experience which slows ordinary movements and turns routine tasks into tortuous events.

28. We are all intensely involved in profiting on the expenses of other people.

29. The contribution of the coalition to the passage of the legislation was capitalized on by the opposition.

30. He is as equally at ease hobnobbing with celebrities as he is relaxing in his own home.

31. These instructions are contingent to your acceptance.

32. The prime minister's reply, he complained, was warm and gratuitous but not very specific.

33. Iago is regarded by all as an honest, truthful man.

34. The character of Nicholas is recognizable to people who really exist in the world.

35. The number of wireless devices offered by these companies are growing.

36. This book about a politician will have a negative effect in terms of the interests of his opponents.

37. The premier has tried to pressurize the legislature to go along with his proposals.

38. After going only a hundred miles the ship was forced to return to its point of origination.

39. You'll also be amazed, too, at our low prices on basic apparel.

40. The new program will cost in the realm of five million dollars.

41. You can expect similar-type amounts of precipitation over the long weekend.

42. The minister said that he would not want to be categorized with respect to a reply to that statement.

43. There was a general consensus in the neighbourhood that ambulance service in the area was frequently inadequate regarding response time.

44. The head waiter subtly inferred that Aamina should stay inside the restaurant.

45. We have to reconsider the proposal in terms of the legal aspects of that situation.

46. I was playing my typical type of game.

47. It seems like he is rather mad at her for daring to try and deceive him.

48. Frodo continuously fretted about the Ring.

49. I denote a real sense of pride here.

50. One must judge the various proposals on an equal basis.

Part VII: Answers

Section 64a–b (1)

1.	cheapskate	miser
2.	chintzy	cheap
3.	con (v.)	cheat
4.	conniption	rage, tantrum, fit
5.	cook up	concoct
6.	crackdown	enforcement
7.	dress down	scold, reprimand
8.	jock	athlete
9.	cute	precocious
10.	ditch	abandon
11.	down the tube	gone
12.	face the music	confront
13.	fall guy	scapegoat
14.	go downhill	decline, deteriorate
15.	high and mighty	haughty
16.	hunch	premonition
17.	jerk	ingrate
18.	miss out	forego, lose an opportunity
19.	on the spot	implicated
20.	scrounge	scavenge
21.	slapdash	hasty
22.	southpaw	lefthander
23.	egghead	intellectual
24.	shocker	surprise
25.	up the creek	in trouble

Section 64a–b (2)

1. Canadians can **greatly benefit from** learning both French and English.
2. Gulliver encounters several **unusual** situations including a land **populated** with **tiny people.**
3. **Suspicious-looking** people **loiter** in the park near my house.
4. At the beginning of *The Taming of the Shrew*, Sly **drinks too much**, falls asleep, and gets **deceived** into thinking he is a nobleman.
5. Characters in the book use hilariously dated phrases **such as** "Twern't me McGee" and "Lay some skin on me Flynn."
6. Juliet**'s beauty** inspires Romeo to perform several **daring** actions.
7. The results of our cloning experiment **differed from the results we anticipated**.

8. We need to analyze the policy decisions before we try **to** develop our plan.

9. The collapse of the market has made selecting stocks **much more difficult**.

10. Mrs. Jellyby's obsession with philanthropy causes her **to ignore** her own children.

Section 64c (1)

[overly pretentious words are marked with an asterisk]

1.	ablutions*	ritual washing
2.	assiduity*	perseverance
3.	bellicose	warlike
4.	cachinnation*	laughter
5.	circumambient*	surrounding
6.	collation	arrangement
7.	colloquy	conversation
8.	comminatory*	threatening
9.	compotation*	drinking party
10.	concatenation*	linkage
11.	confabulate	to converse
12.	conflagration	fire
13.	contumelious*	insulting
14.	crepuscular*	dimly lit
15.	defenestration*	the act of throwing someone out a window
16.	divagation*	digression
17.	doff	take off or tip one's hat
18.	egress	exit
19.	eleemosynary*	charitable
20.	equitation	horsemanship
21.	erstwhile	former, previous
22.	frangible	fragile, breakable
23.	gustatory	taste
24.	habiliments*	clothes
25.	hebdomadal*	weekly
26.	impudicity*	immodesty, shamelessness
27.	ineluctable	irresistible
28.	jejune	dull
29.	lubricity*	slipperiness
30.	lucubrations*	pedantic writings
31.	matutinal	early in the morning
32.	mentation*	mental activity
33.	objurgation*	a rebuke
34.	obloquy*	verbal abuse, disgrace

35.	oppugning*	opposing
36.	orthography	spelling
37.	otiose*	functionless
38.	pellucid	clear
39.	penurious	poor
40.	peregrinations*	travels
41.	propinquity	nearness
42.	raison d'etre	purpose, reason for being
43.	rebarbative*	irritating, unattractive
44.	repast	meal
45.	rubicund	red-faced
46.	salubrious	healthful
47.	sartorial	related to clothing
48.	serendipitous	fortunate
49.	sesquipedalian*	overly long, words of many syllables
50.	superincumbent	lying on top of
51.	tenebrous*	dark, gloomy
52.	transpontine*	across a bridge; also, highly melodramatic (plays)
53.	vilipend*	to disparage, criticize
54.	visage	face
55.	veridical	truthful, realistic
56.	Weltanschauung	world view

Section 64c (2)

1. Donald threw his computer out of the window.
2. Luckily, Sri was able to get the two concert tickets he wanted.
3. People who live in glass houses should not throw stones.
4. Our teacher handed out the examinations and told us not to talk.
5. The prototype has drastically changed from our initial sketches.

Section 66 (1)

1. car – hybrid model – Prius
2. art – painting – modern painting – Picasso's *Guernica*
3. answered – responded – refuted
4. said – observed – criticized
5. food – green vegetable – broccoli
6. drink (v.) – imbibe – sip
7. drink (n.) – hot beverage – specialty coffee – peppermint latte
8. people – young people – child soldiers – child soldiers of Sierra Leone
9. mythical thing – god – Zeus
10. entertainment – movie – classic comedy – *A Night at the Opera*
11. creature – pet – exotic pet – capuchin monkey
12. structure – building – house – bungalow
13. see – inspect – scrutinize
14. moved – walked – strolled
15. concept – idea – philosophy – existentialism
16. freedom – liberty – right – habeas corpus
17. music – contemporary music – jazz

Section 66 (2)

My recently completed Bachelor of Science in Ecology from the University of Alberta and my two years of co-op experience as a junior researcher at the Canadian Centres for Disease Control combine to make me well-suited to meet the needs of your organization. At university, I studied courses in both the arts (scientific writing, research methods) and sciences (including senior seminars in scientific method and laboratory practices); I also presented a paper on Alberta's endangered bird species at an undergraduate research conference and have had my paper accepted for publication in *Habitat Studies*. I have worked for the past six years as a volunteer for the Canadian Wildlife Federation and the David Suzuki Foundation, and my pre–co-op summer employment at Environment Canada, the Workers' Compensation Board of BC, and the Bank of Montreal have given me varied experience working in busy office settings.

Section 67

1. innocent (f), artless (u), crass (u), dense (u), dull (u), dumb (u), feeble-minded (u), foolish (u), green (u), ignorant (u), inept (u), ingenuous (u), naïve (u), obtuse (u), shallow (u), simple (u), slow (u), stupid (u), thick (u), unsophisticated (u), unthinking (u)
2. slender (f), slim (f), svelte (f), trim (f), lanky (n), lean (n), slight (n), spare (n), bony (u), gaunt (u), rawboned (u), scrawny (u), skinny (u), spindly (u), thin (u), twiggy (u), underweight (u), weedy (u)
3. artful (f), diplomatic (f), clever (n), suave (n), crafty (u), cunning (u), devious (u), foxy (u), greasy (u), guileful (u), insinuating (u), oily (u), scheming (u), slimy (u), slippery (u), sly (u), smooth (u), tricky (u), unctuous (u), wily (u)
4. assurance (f), boldness (f), audacity (n), pride (n), arrogance (u), brass (u), brazenness (u), cheek (u), chutzpah (u), effrontery (u), gall (u), highhandedness (u), impertinence (u), impudence (u), insolence (u), nerve (u), presumption (u), temerity (u)
5. genius (f), intellectual (f), sage (f), savant (f), scholar (f), thinker (f), brain (n), brainworker (n), mind (n), pundit (n), bookworm (u), egghead (u), highbrow (u), pedant (u), smarty (u), geek (u)

Section 68

1. strike, lockout
2. tax increase (or pay raise)
3. career criminal
4. prison
5. poor
6. spy satellites
7. under arrest
8. funeral home (mortuary); cemetery
9. lie
10. in wartime, shot by one's fellow soldiers
11. sick, ill
12. storm

Section 69 (1)

1. It was an **incredible** display of manual dexterity.
2. The Office of the Auditor General, **which** is an independent office of the Legislative Assembly, conducts audits.
3. The company's representatives claimed to be **authorities** on the subject.
4. The performance of our local orchestra was spirited and **energetic**.
5. We tried to convince her that her fear was entirely **imaginary**.
6. Some shoppers stopped buying coffee because they found the price so **exorbitant**, if not **astronomical**.
7. The premier of Alberta led his party to the best of his **abilities**.
8. He was **decidedly** on the wrong track with his reserach.
9. The conference is intended to focus attention on the problems facing our **affluent** society.
10. The cat was very **heavy**, weighing over twenty pounds.

Section 69 (2)

1. This Winston Churchill biography describes the context for several of his most famous **quotations**.
2. Being an expatriate in this city carries a certain **cachet**.
3. He was **uninterested** in the side-effects of the experimental treatment.
4. The prince was very **complimentary** of his subjects' efforts.
5. Philanthropy is a central **tenet** of his philosophy.
6. The negative **effects** of high inflation rates were quickly seen in the economy.
7. We were amazed by each of the magician's illusions **except** for the last one.
8. The lawyer's **conscience** prevented her from agreeing to prosecute the case.
9. The **eminent** philosopher has been awarded another honourary doctorate.
10. Kevin was the **past** president of the university's English society.

Section 70 (1)

1. The generation gap between them is **evident in** their uneasiness **over** each other's boredom.
2. Tanya **made us laugh** with stories of her adventures in the Yukon.
3. Last summer I was **given** a scrawny, mangy mutt.
4. Desdemona had unquestioning faith **in** Iago's character.
5. He suggested **that I use** this new product. (OR, He suggested **using** this new product.)
6. The analysis is weak because it **lacks specific details**.
7. I am amazed **by** the report's suggestions.
8. Lovers and poets create dream **worlds which** only they can inhabit.
9. Ironically, although Huck fails, Tom succeeds **in freeing** Jim.
10. She has an unusual philosophy **about** modern technology.
11. We **discussed global warming**.
12. The class **emphasized mathematics skills**.

Section 70 (2)

1. New recruits are trained to conform <u>to</u> the values, code of conduct, and dress code of the armed forces.
2. During the garage sale, Alfonso reluctantly parted <u>with</u> his beloved television.
3. The imam was prohibited, by the oppressive laws of the state, <u>from addressing</u> the crowd of his followers.
4. After the thirteen-year-old received his music scholarship he was entrusted <u>to</u> the care of the academy guardians.
5. The new president's directives are no different <u>from</u> his predecessor's.
6. Make sure the new air conditioner that is purchased for the office complies <u>with</u> the rules about energy use.
7. Our study will provide us with insight <u>into</u> how the lack of green spaces in a city can affect residents.
8. Because of his failure to register on time, Pancho was disqualified <u>from</u> competing in the javelin event.
9. When they were deciding the format of the debate, Caroline and Hana agreed <u>to</u> the theme that Bruce suggested.
10. The new regulations about final examinations are definitely cause <u>for</u> complaint.

Section 71c

1. She told him exactly what she thought of him.
2. Golding's *Lord of the Flies* concerns a group of young boys who revert to savagery.
3. Looking ahead, the economist sees slow growth in the Canadian economy.
4. She approached the door with feelings of dread.
5. He is adventurous, but not reckless.
6. If one doesn't examine the subject thoroughly, one might miss something important.
7. Most people would rather flee danger than face it.
8. Carol realized that she first had to make a careful outline to produce a well-organized

essay.

9. If enough food cannot be supplied for all the people in the world, humankind will have to deal with widespread famine.

10. The singer in the film does not fit the musician stereotype.

Section 71a–c (1)

1. Nature is a powerful image in this poem.
2. Today's courses require more research and thought than the age-old memory work typical of education in the past.
3. These things puzzled him.
4. Advances in information technology make possible greater computerization of machinery.
5. Since he is human, Othello has many faults.
6. Her self-confidence made her strong.
7. The president and the prime minister agree about the future.
8. The playwright also used repetition.
9. Two hundred people pressed against the ropes outside the auditorium.
10. In the past sixth months, I have had to move twice.

Section 71a–c (2)

1. Parents who wish to see a game live and without their children must leave them at home with a babysitter; they end up paying for the sitter as well as the game.
2. At soccer practice, our coach would single out players who performed poorly in passing drills, requiring them to run laps after the practice was over.
3. A surprising number of lawyers and stockbrokers play the game; they thrive on the strategic planning the game requires.

Section 71a–d

Elect me student council president tomorrow! You will be making the right choice for several reasons. First, you will be choosing someone with leadership experience. I was president of both the French Society and the Amateur Entomologist Association last year. Second, you will be choosing someone with experience working with university administration to improve campus life. Because of my efforts on the green panel, the campus has new recycling bins. Third and most important, you will be choosing someone with school spirit. No one loves this school more than me, and I will do all that I can to make this our best year yet.

Section 71e

1. The new business kept Debora very busy.
2. We began working on the server errors at dawn.
3. His campaign never recovered after reporters caught him taking bribes.
4. The Spartans fought with determination to hold back the Persians at Thermopylae.
5. The extruded polymer is very flat.
6. The infection made him severely ill.
7. There is no panacea for this city's problems.

8. Seeing Jehona arrive with Mikhail made Hui-Ying jealous.

9. Ellisabet's success at the blackjack table was fleeting.

10. We need to solve the online fraud problem early.

Section 71g

1.	unacceptable [use *division of tasks*]
2.	unacceptable [use *workers' injuries*]
3.	acceptable, now a commonly used phrase
4.	acceptable, now a very common phrase
5.	acceptable, now a common phrase
6.	acceptable, now a very common phrase
7.	unacceptable [use *planning the use of resources*]
8.	acceptable, a commonly used phrase
9.	acceptable, a commonly used phrase
10.	acceptable, a commonly used phrase
11.	unacceptable [use *organization of staff*]
12.	acceptable, a commonly used phrase
13.	unacceptable [use *coup*, or *change of government*]
14.	acceptable
15.	acceptable, a commonly used phrase
16.	unacceptable [use *a cause of fear*]
17.	acceptable, a commonly used phrase
18.	acceptable, a commonly used phrase
19.	unacceptable [use *overreaction*]
20.	acceptable, a commonly used expression
21.	acceptable in computer-related contexts
22.	unacceptable [use *direct contact*]

Section 72

1. The <u>number</u> of H1N1 flu cases seemed to decrease in the second week.

2. ~~The reason why~~ I am contacting you ~~is~~ because your payment is overdue.

3. The international community has made several diplomatic efforts to resolve the tensions <u>among</u> Liberia, Sierra Leone, and Guinea.

4. Whenever we discuss the problems in our relationship, you seem completely <u>uninterested</u> in anything I have to say.

5. The new policies <u>should have</u> prevented police officers [**or** <u>the police</u>] from making these types of errors.

6. The new advertising campaign was much more <u>distinctive</u> than the one that he originally proposed.

7. There's little we can do, and the murderer was already <u>hanged</u> <u>anyway.</u>

8. After two sleepless nights, Marissa ~~literally~~ fought with her eyes to keep them from closing.

Conserving electricity in your home is **easy** and will **reduce your energy bills. It will also reduce** your environmental impact. One place to start conserving **is** lighting. **An easy first** step is replacing the incandescent bulbs in your home **with** compact fluorescent **lights. T**hese more efficient bulbs **use up to 75% less energy and** will make a **significant** difference over **the year. A**nother place to look for potential savings **is** heating and cooling. The first step is simple: **use** less. In summer, **turn down** your air conditioner—or **turn it off** all together and use a fan instead. In winter, wear an **extra layer** and **turn down the heating. You can also save energy by** replacing your furnace and air conditioner filters every season **and** using curtains or **blinds to** block the sun in the **summer and** retain the **heat in** the **winter.** You can also save energy by **using electronics** more efficiently. **M**any devices such as televisions, stereos, and microwaves **use** electricity even when they are turned "off," **so u**nplugging them when they are not in use can save a surprising amount of **electricity.** These are only a few of the easy steps you can take to save **electricity.** You will be surprised by how quickly small steps add up and **save you money**!

Review exercise: Part VII

1. They discussed the psychiatrist's role in motivating athletes.
2. The team is a close-knit unit.
3. Our strategy is to position union members advantageously.
4. Because this word is repeated throughout the play, it is important.
5. In the winter tourists spend less.
6. Her perfectionism is evident in her business.
7. We hope that this weekend's events will be successful.
8. He did not know how to use the tools properly.
9. One error usually leads to another.
10. This passage is essential in the novel.
11. His metaphors evoke a sinister feeling in the reader.
12. Eliot sees his poems as part of a tradition of knowledge and poetry.
13. She has him at her beck and call.
14. He found himself powerless.
15. I resolved to do my best to make friends and work hard.
16. The hulls of many tankers were ripped open, dumping countless barrels of oil into the sea.
17. Hamlet spends the whole play looking for an opportunity to avenge his father's death.
18. This poem suggests that one should seize the day.
19. He is only in town occasionally.
20. The prime minister is waiting for the premiers to present their demands.
21. Because she gave me so much money, I thanked her profusely.
22. The deal might not have gone ahead if Anderson hadn't been so persistent.
23. In watching these shows or movies, viewers may develop a love of violence.
24. This man thought it was his duty to exact revenge.
25. In Olympic sports, nationalism is becoming increasingly important.
26. She saw that this was the remnant of an important species.
27. For more than a million Canadians, back pain is incapacitating: it slows ordinary

movements and turns routine events into torture.

28. We are all intensely involved in profiting from the expenses of others.

29. The opposition capitalized on the coalition's contribution to the passage of the legislation.

30. He is as comfortable mixing with celebrities as he is relaxing at home.

31. These instructions are contingent upon your acceptance.

32. The prime minister's reply, he complained, was "warm and gracious but not very specific."

33. Iago is regarded by all as an honest man.

34. The character Nicholas is recognizable to real people.

35. The number of wireless devices offered by these companies is growing.

36. This book about a politician will negatively affect his opponents' interests.

37. The premier has tried to pressure the legislature to go along with his proposals.

38. After going only a hundred miles, the ship was forced to return to its point of origin.

39. You'll be amazed, too, at our low prices on basic apparel.

40. The new program will cost approximately five million dollars.

41. You can expect similar amounts of precipitation over the long weekend.

42. The minister said that he had no comment.

43. There was a consensus in the neighbourhood that ambulance service was slow.

44. The head waiter subtly implied that Aamina should stay inside the restaurant.

45. We have to reconsider the legal elements of the proposal.

46. I was playing my typical game.

47. It seems as if he is angry with her for trying to deceive him.

48. Frodo continually fretted about the Ring.

49. I detect a sense of pride here.

50. One must judge the proposals equally.

Part VIII
Research, Writing, and Documentation

Paraphrasing and summarizing
pp. 411–419

Here are two paragraphs from Rupert Brooke's *Letters from America*. For each, write (a) a paraphrase, (b) a paraphrase with some quotation mixed in, and (c) a summary. Include an effective lead-in (attribution) for the material and a parenthetical reference in the MLA style for each piece you write.

(1) Ottawa came as a relief after Montreal. There is no such sense of strain and tightness in the atmosphere. The British, if not greatly in the majority, are in the ascendancy; also, the city seems conscious of other than financial standards, and quietly, with dignity, aware of her own purpose. The Canadians, like the Americans, chose to have for their capital a city which did not lead in population or wealth. This is particularly fortunate in Canada, an extremely individualistic country, whose inhabitants are only just beginning to be faintly conscious of their nationality. Here, at least, Canada is more than the Canadian. A man desiring to praise Ottawa would begin to do so without statistics of wealth and growth of population; and this can be said of no other city in Canada except Quebec. Not that there are not immense lumber-mills and the rest in Ottawa. But the Government farm, and the Parliament buildings, are more important. Also, although the "spoils" system obtains a good deal in this country, the nucleus of the Civil Service is much the same as in England; so there is an atmosphere of Civil Servants about Ottawa, an atmosphere of safeness and honour and massive buildings and well-shaded walks. After all, there is in the qualities of Civility and Service much beauty, of a kind which would adorn Canada. (54–55)

(2) Winnipeg is the West. It is important and obvious that in Canada there are two or three (some say five) distinct Canadas. Even if you lump the French and English together as one community in the East, there remains the gulf of the Great Lakes. The difference between East and West is possibly no greater than that between North and South England, or Bavaria and Prussia; but in this country, yet unconscious of itself, there is so much less to hold them together. The character of the land and the people differs; their interests, as it appears to them, are not the same. Winnipeg is a new city. In the archives at Ottawa is a picture of Winnipeg in 1870—Mainstreet, with a few shacks, and the prairie either end. Now her population is a hundred thousand, and she has the biggest this, that, and the other west of Toronto. A new city; a little more American than the other Canadian cities, but not unpleasantly so. The streets are wider, and full of a bustle which keeps clear of hustle. The people have something of the free swing of Americans, without the bumptiousness; a tempered democracy, a mitigated independence of bearing. The manners of Winnipeg, of the West, impress the stranger as better than those of the East, more friendly, more hearty, more certain to achieve graciousness, if not grace. There is, even, in the architecture of Winnipeg, a sort of gauche pride visible. It is hideous, of course, even more hideous than Toronto or Montreal; but cheerily and windily so. There is no scheme in the city, and no beauty, but it is at least preferable to Birmingham, less dingy, less directly depressing. It has no real slums, even though there is poverty and destitution. (102–03)

Documenting in MLA

pp. 420–446

Using MLA format, create a works-cited list for the following items.

1. A 2007 printed book from the library. It is titled *The West beyond the West: A History of British Columbia*. The author's name is Jean Barman. The publisher is University of Toronto Press, and they are based in Toronto. The book is 480 pages long.

2. An article from the journal, accessed online, called *Journal of Environmental Quality*, by Million B. Woudneh, Ziqing Ou, Mark Sekela, Taina Tuominen, and Melissa Gledhill. The article's title is "Pesticide Multiresidues in Waters of the Lower Fraser Valley, British Columbia" You found the article in issue 3 of volume 38 (pages 940–7), which was published in 2009. You accessed the information on 22 January 2013. The article was located in the Medline database which is published through ProQuest, LLC.

3. A 1942 article from the first issue of volume six in *British Columbia Historical Quarterly*. It is titled "The Chinook Jargon and British Columbia" and was written by Robert Laurence Reid. It was found on pages 1–11. You accessed this title at the library on 15 February 2013 in a printed issue of the journal.

4. An article you read on the *Toronto Star* website on February 16th, 2013. The information was posted on the 10th of January, 2013. The author is Sachin Maharaj, and the article was titled "Imposing contracts on Ontario teachers is bad policy and bad politics." The *Toronto Star* is published by Torstar Corp.

5. Emily Carr's oil-on-canvas painting "Skidegate", which was painted in 1912. You viewed the painting at the Vancouver Art Gallery, located at 750 Hornby Street in Vancouver, British Columbia.

Documenting in APA

pp. 447–466

Using APA format, create a reference list for the following items.

1. A printed book titled *Goths, Gamers, and Grrrls: Deviance and Youth Subcultures.* It is written by Robert Haenfler, who is a professor at the University of Chicago. The book is published on 26th of February, 2013 by University of Texas Press, which is based in Austin, Texas.

2. An article you accessed using the JSTOR database (which does not provide DOI numbers) by Sherry Kleinman and Gary Allen Fine. It is titled "Rethinking Subculture: An Interactionist analysis" and is published in the *American Journal of Sociology* (volume 85, issue 1). It can be found at http://www.jstor.org/stable/2778065

3. An audio podcast episode of the CBC radio program *Tapestry*, which is produced by Elisabeth Bowie. The episode is titled "Prayer: The Small but Mighty," and it was published on 5 January 2013. The CBC is headquartered in Toronto, Ontario.

4. A blog post by Daniel Vidal titled "Save the Date, Help the World" it was added to the website http://www.wholefoodsmarket.com/blog/save-date-help-world in 2013.

5. A fourth edition of the printed book from the library titled *Working People: An Illustrated History of the Canadian Labour Movement.* It is written by Daria Morton and translated from French by Inna Rasitsan. It is published in 1999 by McGill-Queen's University Press, which is based in Montreal, Quebec.

PART VIII: ANSWERS

Section 78

(1) Paraphrase

Rupert Brooke, in his 1916 book *Letters from America*, describes Ottawa as a city that defines Canada and Canadians. He begins by stating that, unlike Montreal, Ottawa has a growing British population who are not necessarily focussed on finances. He continues this theme by comparing Canada to America; he believes they both picked a capital city that is not notable for its population or wealth. This choice, he claims, is a sign of the individualistic quality of a country whose citizens, in other respects individualistic, are starting to take notice of their nationality. He points out that although there is substantial industry in Ottawa, the Government farm and Parliament Buildings take priority in people's minds because they reflect the honourable values of civil service. (Brooke 54–55)

Paraphrase and Quotation

Brooke, in *Letters from America*, expresses "relief" in finding himself in Ottawa after visiting Montreal because Ottawa, even though it is a capital city with industry, does not flaunt its wealth or population growth. He feels that this confidence befits a nation whose citizens are becoming "faintly conscious of their nationality." Civil service is Ottawa's primary concern, and, according to Brooke, "there is in the qualities of Civility and Service much beauty." (Brooke 54–55)

Summary

Brooke describes Ottawa as a fitting capital for Canadians. Not obsessed with distinctions such as wealth or population growth, despite its industries, Ottawa focuses on the single purpose of civil service. He claims that the qualities and institutions of this civil service lends an aura of safety and beauty to the city. (Brooke 54–55)

(2) Paraphrase

In his *Letters from America*, Brooke describes Winnipeg as different from cities in eastern Canada. Winnipeg, according to Brooke, represents the qualities of the West: a fast-growing energetic city that, like an American city, has wide streets and an extroverted population. He notes how the city's architecture, despite its ugliness, conveys Winnipeggers' pride and satisfaction even though there is evidence of poverty in their city. (Brooke 102–03)

Paraphrase and Quotation

"Winnipeg is the West." So announces Rupert Brooke in his *Letters from America*. He feels that Winnipeg is different from other cities in Canada, a country "yet unconscious of itself." Within this struggle for identity, Brooke sees Winnipeg as a new and fast-growing city that is more American than Canadian but "not unpleasantly so." Streets are wider and the people "more friendly, more hearty, more certain to achieve graciousness" than their counterparts in Canada and America. Although the architecture is "hideous" and poverty exists, the city is cheerful. (Brooke 102–03)

Summary

Brooke believes Winnipeg represents the west. He describes it as a new, fast-growing city similar to American cities with wide streets and extroverted people who take pride in their city and its architecture. He acknowledges that there is some poverty in the city. (Brooke 102–03)

Works Cited

Barman, Jean. *The West beyond the West: A History of British Columbia.* Toronto: University of Toronto Press, 2007. Print.

Carr, Emily. *Skidegate.* 1912. Oil on Canvas. Vancouver Art Gallery, Vancouver.

Maharaj, Sachin. "Imposing contracts on Ontario teachers is bad policy and bad politics." *thestar.ca.* Torstar, 10 Jan. 2013. Web. 16 Feb. 2013.

Reid, Robert Laurence. "The Chinook Jargon and British Columbia." *British Columbia Historical Quarterly* 6.1 (1942): 1–11. Print.

Woudneh, Million B., et al. "Pesticide Multiresidues in Waters of the Lower Fraser Valley, British Columbia." *Journal of Environmental Quality.* 38.3 (2009): 940–947. *Medline.* ProQuest, 2009. Web. 22 January 2013.

References

Bowie, E. (producer). (2013, January 5). Prayer: The small but mighty [Audio podcast episode]. In Tapestry. Retrieved from http://www.cbc.ca/tapestry/podcasts/

Fine, G. A., & Kleinman, S. (1978). Rethinking subculture: An interactionist analysis. American Journal of Sociology, 85(1). 1-20. Retrieved from http://www.jstor.org/stable/2778065

Haenfler, R. (2013). Goths, gamers, and grrrls: deviance and youth subcultures. Austin, TX: University of Texas Press.

Morton, D. (1999). Working people: An illustrated history of the Canadian labour movement (4th ed.). (I. Rasitsan, Trans.). Montreal, QU: McGill-Queen's University Press.

Vidal, D. (2013). Save the date, help the world [Web log post]. Retrieved from http://www.wholefoodsmarket.com/blog/save-date-help-world

Notes

Notes